Praise for
The *Finding Meaning* Workbook

"In this deeply empathic, accessible, intuitive, and affirming workbook, David Kessler gives us the opportunity to create our own personal roadmap for finding meaning while navigating grief, reminding us that we will all experience loss and that there is no 'wrong way' to grieve. The exercises and prompts are universally useful for a person navigating any kind of loss and gently guide us back to the possibilities of healing and meaning-making in the wake of loss and grief."

—Ramani Durvasula, PhD, clinical psychologist, professor emerita of psychology, and author of the *New York Times* bestselling book *It's Not You: Identifying and Healing from Narcissistic People*

"David Kessler shows us that dealing with emotions attached to grief and loss will help us find comfort, hope, and healing. The *Finding Meaning* workbook provides gentle, expert guidance through the twists and turns of the grieving process, leading to the last place we expect to arrive: a place where strength, clarity, and purpose can grow."

—Frank Anderson, MD, author of *To Be Loved* and *Transcending Trauma*

"David Kessler offers us a kind, empowering, and life-changing guide to help any of us who are grieving the loss of a loved one. This workbook provides practical steps to move through the stages of grief in our own way, finding strength, clarity, and meaning by being open to the full spectrum of emotions that come with loss. With inspiring stories and practical exercises, these pages are a soothing companion in our moving forward with an expanded embracing of life's purpose and loving relationships."

—Daniel J. Siegel, MD, *New York Times* bestselling author of *Aware, IntraConnected,* and *Personality and Wholeness in Therapy* and executive director of the Mindsight Institute

Also by David Kessler

Finding Meaning: The Sixth Stage of Grief

Healing Grief Card Deck: 55 Practices to Find Peace

*You Can Heal Your Heart: Finding Peace After a Breakup,
Divorce, or Death* (coauthor with Louise Hay)

*Visions, Trips, and Crowded Rooms: Who
and What You See Before You Die*

*On Grief and Grieving: Finding the Meaning
of Grief Through the Five Stages of Loss*
(coauthor with Elisabeth Kübler-Ross)

*Life Lessons: Two Experts on Death and Dying
Teach Us About the Mysteries of Life and Living*
(coauthor with Elisabeth Kübler-Ross)

*The Needs of the Dying: A Guide for Bringing
Hope, Comfort, and Love to Life's Final Chapter*

Finding Meaning

The Sixth
Stage of Grief
Workbook

Finding Meaning

The Sixth
Stage of Grief
Workbook

Tools for Releasing Pain and Remembering with Love

DAVID KESSLER

Finding Meaning: The Sixth Stage of Grief Workbook
Copyright © 2024 by David Kessler

Published by
Bridge City Books, an imprint of PESI Publishing, Inc.
3839 White Ave
Eau Claire, WI 54703

Cover and interior design by Emily Dyer
Editing by David Hochman

ISBN 9781962305297 (print)
ISBN 9781962305303 (ePUB)
ISBN 9781962305310 (ePDF)

Bridge City Books

Table of Contents

A Message from David

If you're reading this workbook, you are probably dealing with loss in some way. Wherever you are in your experience with grief, let me begin by saying how grateful I am that you're here, and also how heartbreaking it is that you're here. I truly wish we could be together on these pages for any other reason. My sincerest hope is that the reflections and exercises ahead can bring you peace and help you find comfort.

My heart is so touched by how *Finding Meaning* has resonated with people around the world. Readers often tell me how much the book has helped, and also how it makes them want to explore this work even further. At the same time, there are people who see the title and tell me they're not quite there yet. "I'm in the pain and not ready to find meaning," they say. That's when I remind them that *Finding Meaning* is a book about excavating the pain. That is also the point of the workbook you're holding. This is a place for you to explore and map out your pain as we discover together the meaning underneath.

Digging into the pain won't be easy. It certainly wasn't for me. When I began working on *Finding Meaning*, I had no idea how personal and emotional writing the book would be. As a grief expert, my decades of experience with people on the tenderest edges of life and death had acquainted me with grief. I was privileged to be a student and learn from my coauthor and mentor Elisabeth Kübler-Ross, whose groundbreaking book *On Death and Dying* identified the five stages of dying and changed the way people around the world think and talk about the final stages of life. My mentor and I eventually wrote two books together, and for our second, *On Grief and Grieving*, which was Elisabeth's last, she asked me to help adapt her five stages (that she had observed in the dying) to account for similar stages we both recognized in those who are grieving. The five stages identified by Elisabeth Kübler-Ross are denial, anger, bargaining, depression, and acceptance™.

Like the stages of death and dying, the stages of grief were never meant to be prescriptive. As I often say, they describe, not prescribe. Messy emotions do not fit into neat packages. Both my parents had died, as well as a nephew, who was like a brother. With these losses, my grief did not follow an orderly progression. Even with the fifth stage of acceptance, my journey with grief continued.

Nothing, however, prepared me for the shattering loss I experienced with the unexpected death of my 21-year-old son, David. So all-consuming was the pain, I thought I might never write again or lecture again or, frankly, want to live again. That is a decision that every person in grief makes consciously or unconsciously. It was a choice that felt so real to me. I live on a sweet, tree-lined street full of lovely little houses. But it was easy to imagine a future in which two teenagers might ride by, pointing at one home in disrepair and covered in cobwebs. "Is that house haunted?" one might say. The other would reply, "No it's an old man who never comes out. He was a grief expert, but then his own son died." Yes, I could become that guy or I could at some point live again.

After David's death I wasn't ready to surface from the despair. But even then, I knew that I must continue to live, not only for my surviving son, but also for my own sake. I refused to allow David's death to be meaningless or to continue on with my own life without a sense of meaning. I had no idea what I would do to wrest meaning from this terrible time. But I knew I couldn't and wouldn't stop at acceptance. There had to be something more.

People often ask what I did to persevere and to find meaning in the midst of inescapable pain—because I did eventually find meaning. For me, it didn't happen by pushing through the pain or pushing the pain aside. Rather, it was by allowing myself to live in the pain. The pain was part of why I kept going. It was what made me want to be of service to others, and to honor David's life. What I often say is that pain from loss is inevitable. Suffering is optional. You may remember that idea from *Finding Meaning*, but it's worth repeating as we begin this workbook together. I cannot take away your pain. It's not my place to do that. Your pain is yours. It's part of the love you feel. What I can do, however, is remind you that if you look for meaning, your pain will change, your suffering will lessen.

This workbook is designed to help you in your search for meaning. Whether you've faced the death of a child, spouse, sibling, parent, grandparent, or other loved one, or are supporting others in their grief as a trusted friend, clinician, or counselor, there is space here to look closer at the meaning of loss, to ask deeper questions and find deeper answers. As I said, this work will be challenging. In our instant gratification world, we often want to speed through the pain and get to the meaning. But it doesn't work that way. If you put this workbook down, the pain will not disappear. You still walk with it, feel it, reckon with grief's magnitude. Only by excavating the pure emotion will you find love on the other side of pain. And it is in that love where we find meaning, the sixth stage of grief.

Before we begin, allow me to share again some thoughts from *Finding Meaning* that may guide you in your process:

1. Meaning is relative and personal.

2. Meaning takes time. You may not find it until months or even years after loss.

3. Meaning doesn't require understanding. It's not necessary to understand why someone died in order to find meaning.

4. Even when you do find meaning, you won't feel it was worth the cost of what you lost.

5. Your loss is not a test, a lesson, something to handle, a gift, or a blessing. Loss is what happens to you in life. Meaning is what *you* make happen after loss.

6. Only you can find your own meaning.

7. Meaningful connections will heal painful memories.

So many of us feel powerless in grief—that it's something that's been done to us. With this workbook, my wish for you is to regain your footing and locate new strength. To discover clarity and perspective on the story of your loss. And to find purpose when and where you can. Grief heals the more we engage with it. I hope that by engaging with this material, together we can find meaning wherever and however you can.

It is my privilege to be on this path with you.

—David Kessler

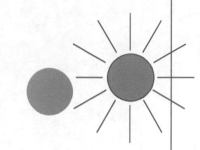

PART 1

The Power of Your Grief

Where Loss Leaves You

Honoring Your Unique Experience in Grief

> "Our own version of our loved one's death—
> the story we tell ourselves about it—can either
> help us heal or keep us mired in suffering."
>
> —*Finding Meaning*

At one of my grief workshops, two women around the same age shared stories of losing their siblings. The first woman told us through sobs about her sister's death from cancer. "She was my best friend, the person I trusted more than anyone else on earth. I really don't see a future without her," she said. The second woman's brother had been murdered. "My whole world changed that day," the woman said, but with a different type of emotion in her eyes. "Ever since, I've been committed 100 percent to stopping violence at any cost."

Two women, two overwhelming losses, two completely different experiences. Our grief is as unique as our fingerprints. One person's loss finds them at the bottom of a pit of pain. Another sees death as a prompt for meaning, action, and forward motion. It's how we react to death that makes the difference between suffering and resilience, and between trauma and transformation.

The grieving mind often finds no hope after loss, but I want you to know that the potential for meaning is ever-present in our lives. The Austrian Holocaust survivor and psychiatrist Victor Frankl suggested that when we are faced with a situation that appears unchangeable, "we are challenged to change ourselves." By making the choice to do that, we can turn tragedy into an occasion for growth.

This workbook is designed to help you gradually, slowly, kindly, gently, work through your pain to find meaning and new ways not just to go through loss but also to grow through it. The point of these exercises isn't to force you to find meaning but, rather, to know that days in despair don't have to be your eternal destiny. This doesn't mean your grief will get smaller over time. It means that you must get bigger. The experience of loss has an amazing power to transform us if we allow it.

But again, every loss is different. That's why the first part of this book is about honoring your unique experience with grief. As I write in *Finding Meaning*, one of my mantras is: "It's your job to honor your own grief. No one else can ever understand it." Because no one else had the special relationship you did with your loved one. Only you know what you're going through. But sometimes you must reexamine fundamental assumptions around grief, particularly if you're feeling stuck in some way. If you think you shouldn't be grieving or have no right to grieve, that will shape your grief. If you think grief is a weakness; if your family or friends think you shouldn't be grieving anymore; if society says you should be over it; if you see your grief as pathetic, as a sign of weakness, or as a losing battle—all that has an impact on your perspective and on your healing process. Our thinking about grief is how we make meaning, and that's why our first task here is to look at the perceptions, feelings, sensations, and stories you have around loss.

The Timeline of Grief

How long has it been? That's often the first question I ask after someone in grief has shared their story. In my online groups and at my retreats and workshops, I want to know how much time has passed since the loss of a loved one. It's not because there is some invisible timeline to grief. It's my way of asking, "How long have you had to process the pain?"

But there isn't a timetable after losing someone.

One of the most common questions I get is "How long am I going to grieve?" Or "How long is my sister or my friend or my husband going to grieve?" My answer is always "How long is the person who died going to be dead? Because if they're going to be dead for a long time, you are going to grieve for a long time." It doesn't mean you will always grieve with pain. To me, one of the goals is, in time, at your own pace, in your own way, you can learn to grieve with more love than pain.

Unfortunately, there's so much judgment around our grief—from society, from family, from others who have not had a loss. These judgments get in the way of the grieving process, particularly when we're judging ourselves. *It's been a year! Why am I still crying? It's been five years. Why am I not over this yet?* So many times we think we should be in a different place than we are. That's why I want to begin with an exercise that considers where you are in your grief. This isn't about the weeks, months, or years since your loved one died. Think of this as a measure of your relationship with grief itself.

Where are you in grief? From the list below, put a check mark by one or more statements you believe about your grief:

☐ My grief hasn't hit me yet.

☐ Time will not change this pain.

☐ Grief is right on time.

☐ I should be over grief by now.

☐ My grief is lasting too long.

☐ I'm stuck in grief.

☐ It's time to move on.

☐ I'm backsliding in grief.

☐ My grief is healing.

☐ My grief has become manageable.

☐ Grief is part of me but doesn't define me.

Let's do that again, but this time, put a check mark by where you think you *should* be in your grief:

❏ My grief hasn't hit me yet.	❏ It's time to move on.
❏ Time will not change this pain.	❏ I'm backsliding in grief.
❏ Grief is right on time.	❏ My grief is healing.
❏ I should be over grief by now.	❏ My grief has become manageable.
❏ My grief is lasting too long.	
❏ I'm stuck in grief.	❏ Grief is part of me but doesn't define me.

Finally, put a check mark by what you think others (friends, family, society) believe about your grief:

❏ My grief hasn't hit me yet.	❏ It's time to move on.
❏ Time will not change this pain.	❏ I'm backsliding in grief.
❏ Grief is right on time.	❏ My grief is healing.
❏ I should be over grief by now.	❏ My grief has become manageable.
❏ My grief is lasting too long.	
❏ I'm stuck in grief.	❏ Grief is part of me but doesn't define me.

It's interesting to notice how those check marks match up, or don't match up, based on judgments. If the responses above are in sync or out of sync, think about what's causing that. Are you telling yourself your grief isn't where it should be due to some preconceived notion about how this process works? Have the people weighing in on your grief experienced grief the same way you are? For instance, is your sister telling you it's time to move on as a widow when, in fact, her husband is still alive? If so, that matters. It reminds me of a quote from the poet Rumi: "If you embark on a journey, don't ask directions from someone who has never left home." Only you know what you're going through, so take a minute to reflect on anything that surprised you in identifying "where you are" in your grief. How does your current status with grief differ from the "shoulds" both inside you and around you?

_____

_____

_____

_____

_____

_____

_____

_____

_____

_____

Meet the Gang of Feelings

Knowing where you are in grief is the first step in honoring and recognizing your unique experience. Your relationship with your loss isn't what your spouse or sibling or friend says it should be, or what the outside world expects it to be. You don't want anyone to lessen your experience or reframe it or tell you to get over it. But you also don't want to find yourself stuck in grief, perpetually feeling yesterday's feelings today. That's why it's so important to identify and understand what you're feeling in the here and now, separate from what the people around you or the world are telling you. When outside influences override our authentic feelings, we lose touch with ourselves and can go numb or become confused.

As you may recall from *Finding Meaning*, you can't heal what you don't feel. But healing requires you to *know* what you're feeling. And with grief, connecting with your feelings can be scary. Most people are afraid of what I call "the gang of feelings." Gangs intimidate us. They lurk, waiting for you to crack open the door so they can break in. Picture this gang: its members are anger, sadness, numbness, yearning, shock, and a lot of other perceived hurtful emotions. The fear is that once you open the door to the gang, they will rush in and overwhelm you, and you'll never be able to free yourself of them. People in fear of this gang often say things like "If I start crying, I'll never stop." But crying, just like everything else in this life, does end. If you can allow yourself to feel the pain in all its depths and cry it out, you might feel very sad, but you won't be overwhelmed by it. Instead, that feeling will move through you and you will be done with it. I'm not saying that you'll never again feel pain over the death of your loved one. You will. But you gave that particular moment of pain its due. You didn't resist it and you won't have to keep reliving it.

We fear the gang of feelings because we never let ourselves experience the entire emotion. Instead, we have emotions about our emotions. We begin to feel sad, and then we feel guilty that we're sad because someone else has it worse, which snaps us out of the sadness before we feel it completely. Or we're angry and we judge our anger, so we move into self-recrimination. Or we're sad but we think we should feel grateful. And on and on. I encourage people to stay with the first generation of emotions, and that's what I want you to do here. Ignore the comments your mind is making about your feelings and try to identify the emotions that arise most naturally and most often for you. This process takes time, and it might feel hard, but as I tell people in my grief work, nothing's ever going to be as hard as what you've already lived through.

For this exercise, use the following feelings wheel for clarity and inspiration.

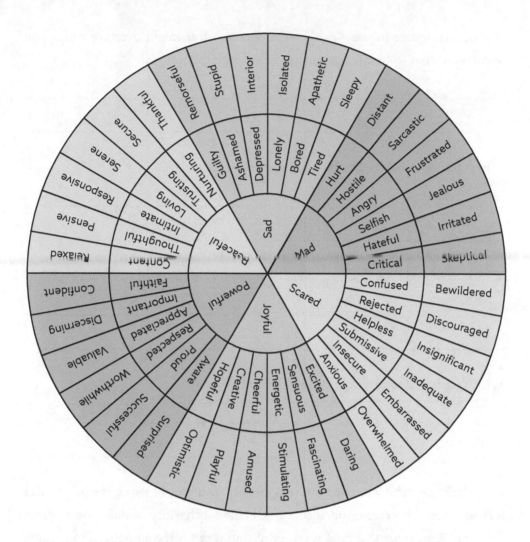

Choosing from the wheel, which three or four feelings best describe your state of mind since your loved one died?

_____

_____

Which feelings are in your "gang"—the ones you fear might overtake you if you opened the door to your truest and most challenging emotions?

_____

_____

Which feelings best describe how you truly feel today?

_____

_____

Which feelings do you find yourself most frequently avoiding or stuffing away?

_____

_____

Which feelings do you currently find hardest to access?

_____

_____

Now, let's take this exercise one step further and think about the ways your feelings might be disguising themselves behind behaviors, actions, or ways of thinking. Remember that grief is powerful, and it can make an impact, sometimes unconsciously, whether that's by pulling you away from people close to you, self-sabotage, blaming others, or self-blame.

Consider how your gang of feelings bullies you to react in specific ways. For this next exercise, you'll identify how different feelings typically make you react. The following are examples of reactions you might experience.

Reactions List	
• Cry uncontrollably	• Overeat
• Question my loyalty	• Meditate or pray
• Talk to someone close to me	• Focus on being in the moment
• Lose myself in memorabilia, old photos, etc.	• Catastrophize (assume the worst)
• Exercise	• Find ways to help others
• Try to fix it	• Ruminate about what-ifs
• Stuff the feeling away	• Indulge in substances (alcohol, drugs, nicotine, etc.)
• Isolate myself	
• Engage in risky behavior (fast driving, casual sex, etc.)	• Deny myself pleasure
	• Beat myself up
• Lash out at others	• Busy myself with work or activities
• Dull my senses (scroll online, watch TV, play video games, watch porn, etc.)	
	• Blame other people
	• Bottle up my emotions
• Go numb	• Say I don't deserve it

In each of the following lines, choose a feeling from the feelings wheel on page 9, then write down how you typically react to that feeling. You can choose from the list above or name your own reaction. As you do, notice how easy it is to mask or sidestep your true feelings by reacting in certain ways. I've provided a few examples first.

When I'm feeling _optimistic_ ,

I tend to _say I don't deserve it_ .

When I'm feeling _bored_ ,

I tend to _busy myself with work or activities_ .

When I'm feeling _scared_ ,

I tend to _bottle up my emotions_ .

When I'm feeling _____ ,

I tend to _____ .

When I'm feeling _____ ,

I tend to _____ .

When I'm feeling _____ ,

I tend to _____ .

When I'm feeling _____ ,

I tend to _____ .

When I'm feeling _____ ,

I tend to _____ .

When I'm feeling _____ ,

I tend to _____ .

When I'm feeling _____ ,

I tend to _____ .

Old Wounds into Cherished Wounds

Whatever you're feeling, you're not feeling the wrong thing. Grief surfaces every imaginable emotion, and anything that comes up for you is okay. I always remind people that death is part of the story for every person who's ever lived. We all come from a long line of dead people. Rest assured, your soul, your psyche, knows how to get through this. Grief is part of the human condition. Above all, know that grief is love. It's a reflection of a connection that we believe has been lost. Sometimes we think we shouldn't grieve someone we had a complicated relationship with. But the reality is, we grieve those we love, those we like, those we dislike, even those we hate. We don't, however, grieve people we're indifferent to. Getting to our first-generation feelings is our way to reckon with the enormity of what happened and to experience loss fully so we can eventually move through the pain.

But when we're in grief, it's helpful to know that old wounds can arise even if the loss feels like nothing we've experienced before. Old wounds, trauma, and childhood events shape who we are and how we process our grief today. My colleague Dr. Edith Eger, a psychologist and Holocaust survivor, says, "In time, our traumatic wounds can become our cherished wounds." But without addressing them, old wounds don't go away. If you've ever asked, "Why am I broken?" or have thoughts like "I'm just damaged" or "I can never heal from this," that's probably an old wound talking. Is it helpful to discount yourself as permanently damaged? Almost never. A better question than "What's wrong with me?" is "What happened to me?"

For this exercise, I want you to take a moment to think not about the person you are now—the person in grief—but, rather, the scared or confused child within you, the person who could probably benefit from a dose of self-compassion. Thinking back through the years to childhood, what old wounds do you carry that may be informing, and possibly interfering with, your healing today? Again, the answer I'm looking for here is *in your childhood*. When was the first time you felt hopeless, damaged, unhealable, broken, wrong, not enough, or "too much"?

_____

_____

_____

_____

_____

_____

We've all had pain and grief modeled for us. Were you told that crying wasn't allowed? Was grieving something people did in silence or in the privacy of hidden sorrow? Did those around you avoid asking for help? Did your family mourn (or skip mourning) in ways that have left you feeling rudderless and without direction in your grief today?

Please share your thoughts on how the way grief was modeled impacts you now. What family beliefs, or societal beliefs, around grief might be coloring the way you're feeling about grief in this moment, whether it's about expectations, values, or experiences that predate the loss of your loved one?

Example: My family never talked about the negative, so I try to stay positive, which often causes me to stuff my feelings.

_____

_____

_____

_____

Now write about how your experience with grief and your healing process today might be different if you could accept yourself for these ancient scars, rather than acting in response to them. In short, how can you turn old wounds into cherished wounds? Note: This exercise can be difficult emotionally. It sometimes helps to think about what the kindest person you know might say to that scared child within, and then channel that person's voice.

Example: *If I were kinder to myself, I would see my grief as normal and natural.*

_____

_____

_____

_____

_____

Your Assumptions Checklist

As you are discovering, your assumptions about grief are based on many factors: what friends and family members expect from you, what the world expects, how you experienced grief or trauma earlier in life, and more. How we think about grief is how we make meaning from grief, which is why I'm having you investigate your beliefs about loss from multiple angles. I'd like you to think about several important parts of your life growing up and what messages were conveyed to you, directly or indirectly.

Example: My family believed grief _should be hidden_   .

My family believed grief _____

_____.

My religion or clergy believed grief _____

_____.

The movies and TV shows I watched suggested that grief _____

_____ .

Society told me that grief _____

_____ .

Tuning into Shame

In a culture where people tend to put a polished gloss on everything (I'm looking at you, social media), it can be easier to bottle up your sadness and pain than to tell someone you're grieving. I understand that completely. After my son David died, if I ran into someone at a party who I hadn't seen in a while, and they asked, "How are the kids?" just as we were ready to jump up and yell "surprise," I wouldn't say, "Oh, well, one kid is grieving and the other one is dead." There's a time and a place for every conversation. Not every situation deserves our grief story.

When someone dies, we tend to think it's because something went wrong, and it's not uncommon to feel shame about it. Or we'll compare our lives to those of others. Perhaps your wife died from early onset Alzheimer's and your neighbor is telling you about the around-the-world anniversary cruise he just went on with his spouse. "Oh, great. What went wrong in *my* life," you might think, "that made things go sideways like this?" It's part of grief to acknowledge that life didn't turn out the way you expected. Your husband ate badly and didn't take care of his health. Now he's dead. Your 20-year-old got in a car after drinking too much and died in a highway accident. What you need to remember in any situation like this is that bad things happen to us without it being because we did something wrong. Death happens, but it doesn't need to be our fault. Loss happens to good people, to bad people, in close-knit families, and in estranged ones. It happens to the rich and to the poor.

As part of this chapter on excavating feelings, I'd like you to reflect on ways you might be hiding your emotions. How freely do you share your truth in different situations? When and with whom do you hide your grief, and when are you more open and honest? Mark the spot on the continuum below that shows where you are with your truth. Try not to judge yourself as you answer. One of our tasks in grief is to protect ourselves and to find support where and when we can.

I'm private with my grief	I'm completely open about my grief

When meeting strangers

←--→

At work

←--→

With my partner

←--→

With my closest friends

←--→

With friends I haven't seen in a while

←--→

With a therapist

←--→

At my place of worship

←--→

With a grief group

←--→

In this workbook

←--→

Notice that last option. I want to make sure you're staying honest with your work here, although I understand that being truthful with yourself about grief can be painful. Take a few minutes to share any insights gained by looking at where you share your grief and whom you choose to share it with. Do you see patterns? Are you able to express yourself with strangers more than with friends? Is your grief group the only place where you can be truly open about your feelings? Shame is closely related to secrecy. What does this exercise tell you about shame you might be feeling?

_____

_____

_____

_____

_____

The Story of Your Loss

Like any story, the story of loss shifts based on where we attach the meaning. You can describe an object on your desk as a piece of wood. But if someone tells you it's a pencil, then the meaning has changed. Now, you can write a novel with it. You can do math with it. With your grief story, it's the same. Death can't just happen, so we must look for ways to explain it, frame it, understand it, assign blame to it. That's why we'll take several opportunities in this workbook to look at the story of your loss to see what's true and what's not, what's useful and what's keeping you from releasing pain.

Before I ask you to tell your story, I want you to take an honest inventory of your beliefs around grief and loss. The following checklist can help you find obstacles as well as pathways as you work toward healing. By noticing various beliefs in yourself—limiting, useful, punishing, motivating—you start to see where there's room for growth and room for reevaluation. Put a check mark next to the statements that best characterize your thoughts in the here and now of your grief. Be very honest!

- ❏ My life cannot be whole without the person I've lost.
- ❏ I'm being disloyal if I heal.
- ❏ I'm being disloyal if I release the pain.
- ❏ If I hold on to an emotion (anger, sadness, etc.), I'll keep their memory alive.
- ❏ I'm not healed yet, but I know I will be one day.
- ❏ Grieving is a weakness.
- ❏ I should be over this.
- ❏ I should feel more emotion than I do.
- ❏ I'm being too hard on myself.
- ❏ I must stop talking about my grief.
- ❏ I'm too much for people.
- ❏ If I push the feelings aside, I can get back to life.
- ❏ I'm not enough (for the world, for my family, etc.).
- ❏ I know deep down that things will be okay.

- ❏ I can't rely on anyone.
- ❏ I just want things to go back to how they were.
- ❏ Nobody understands what I'm going through.
- ❏ I'm a burden.
- ❏ I can make a positive difference in people's lives.
- ❏ I deserve the bad things that happened to me.
- ❏ If I stay busy, I might not notice the pain.
- ❏ I want to make my loved one proud of the life I'm living.
- ❏ If I've come this far, I can survive anything.
- ❏ I don't deserve to be here.
- ❏ I know hope is out there even if I can't see it.
- ❏ I don't see a future.
- ❏ There is life beyond loss.

Take a look at your list and see what's negative and what's positive. Are there ways of thinking that you might want to let go of? Did anything feel more optimistic or more hopeful than you expected? Which statements are clearly holding you back from releasing pain and allowing growth? Are there any giving you comfort or self-compassion as you run through the list? Take a moment to write about your assumptions and which thoughts are serving you and which you'd love to move away from.

_____

_____

_____

_____

_____

Witnessing Your Grief

I often say that meaning both begins and ends with the stories we tell. We all have a stock of stories that explain who we are, what we think, what we dream about, what we fear, what family has meant to us, and what we've accomplished. Having those stories to tell is part of being human. We tell them all the time to family, friends, and strangers. But we also tell stories to ourselves, and when we do, the way we frame them has the power to change our feelings.

In my grief groups and programs, I often ask people to write about their loved ones' deaths. This practice has been inspired, in part, by the work of social psychologist James Pennebaker of the University of Texas. He knew that people who experienced a traumatic event were more depressed, were more emotionally volatile, and died of cancer and heart disease at higher rates than those who had not experienced a traumatic event, which didn't surprise him. What did surprise him was that people who kept their trauma a secret experienced significantly higher rates of death than those who had spoken about it. This made him wonder whether sharing secrets would improve their health. It turned out that they didn't even have to share their secrets with others to benefit. Simply writing them down had a positive effect. His research showed that they went to the doctor less often, lowered their blood pressure, and had better (lower) heart rates. They also had fewer feelings of anxiety and depression.

I can testify from my personal experience how helpful this can be. Telling the story of my grief has helped me work through the resentment, anger, and victimhood that complicated my feelings. And I've seen over and over in my programs how useful it is for people to share the story of their loss, regardless of whether the death happened weeks ago, months ago, or decades ago. As I wrote in *Finding Meaning*, what everyone has in common is that no matter how they grieve, they share a need for their grief to be witnessed.

As we approach the end of this chapter, I want you to share the story of your loss. Even if you've told the story a hundred times, even if your friends or family can't bear to hear it again, even if *you* think you're done telling it, I want you to tell it again. All losses are to be grieved and witnessed.

So, what's your story? Use the following space to tell the story of what happened, how it happened, and how you felt. There are no rules here. The point is to tell the story of your loss with vulnerability and honesty, to get it down on the page, without judgment or reserve, without comparing or minimizing. This is the story of your loss as only you can tell it.

What is the story of your loss?

_____

_____

_____

_____

_____

_____

_____

_____

_____

_____

_____

_____

_____

_____

_____

_____

_____

_____

_____

_____

_____

_____

That's your story, the one you carry with you. But I know from my grief work that telling the story often isn't enough. Sometimes we want other people to "get" our story. That leads to our next exercise. Thinking about the story of your grief, which parts of the narrative do you feel have been witnessed—that is, truly understood—by the people around you? The basic facts? Your deepest emotions? The whole deal?

What have people witnessed about your grief story?

_____

_____

_____

_____

_____

_____

Now write about what people *have not* witnessed. Which parts of your story do you wish people would see and understand that they don't? Which aspects do you keep hidden? In short, in what ways is the story of your grief unwitnessed?

_____

_____

_____

_____

_____

_____

MEANINGFUL REFLECTION

Having grief witnessed is important and powerful. As we end this chapter, take a few minutes to explore what you've learned about yourself and your grief from having it witnessed, by proxy, in this workbook. What new feelings have emerged? What's surprising you? How does looking at the story of your loss change by exploring it from different angles? In the next chapter, we'll continue to think about the story of your grief in new ways and from fresh perspectives. For now, take time to write about the meaning your loss is giving you right now (or the lack of meaning).

_____

_____

_____

_____

_____

_____

_____

_____

_____

2

Questioning the Story
New Perspectives on Your Grief Narrative

> "The story you tell yourself repeatedly
> becomes your meaning."
>
> —*Finding Meaning*

Meaning doesn't happen all at once. As I mentioned, you may not find it until months or even years after loss. But I hope that by doing these exercises, you can begin to recognize opportunities to bring meaning into your life. Living with meaning is a way to honor the person you are mourning; it honors their life, their death, their love, their knowing you, and the time you shared together. Only you can set the pace for this process, but I'm here to offer some ideas and to help guide you on your path with some of the most meaningful exercises I know.

Healing takes time. A woman at a grief workshop once said that after her husband died, she felt like she would never see beyond the pain. She told us it was her fate to be in pain for the rest of her days. It hadn't been long—a few months— since her husband's death. But I told her what I often tell people, which is that pain doesn't need to be your eternal destiny. Again, that doesn't mean your grief gets smaller over time. It means that you must get bigger. As the saying goes, "No mud, no lotus." The most beautiful flower grows out of the mud. Our worst moments can be the seeds of our meaning. They have an amazing power to transform us.

Those brighter moments come by thinking about your grief in new ways. People who have experienced the death of someone close to them sometimes hold narratives in their head that keep them stuck in place and disguise their authentic realities. In the last chapter, you told the story of your loss. Now I'd like you to consider whether that is the only version of the story. In grief, we often create stories to protect ourselves or to avoid pain, but what if those stories are faulty and not serving us? What if they fail to tell the whole story?

To make meaning, sometimes we need to question the stories we have been telling ourselves. Is the story of your grief constrained by "always/never" thinking? By what-ifs or if-onlys? By anxiety? By shame? Is it possible to adjust an angle of your story to bring new insight to what happened or to be gentler with yourself? I like to say that these questions are a way to "test" your grief narrative, and that's an essential step toward finding meaning. Otherwise, the faults in your story can color every choice, every decision, everything you're doing that keeps you locked in loss.

Grief is about our heart, but our mind can take over and get in the way. It's important to acknowledge that. When we experience a loss, our thinking can become rigid or clouded. We see hard facts where there might be room for interpretation. Many times, people blame themselves or blame others for contributing to the death in some way, even if the evidence isn't there to support those charges. Our minds are powerful, and so are the stories we create to make sense of the complicated world. In the pages ahead, I'd like you to examine your grief story to make sure it doesn't need to be edited for accuracy in some way.

Three Stories, Multiple Perceptions

Testing stories about grief is a big part of what I do at my programs. I often use an exercise my friend and author Neil Strauss shared with me. I'll pair people up and ask them to name three major events in their lives—some good, some bad. I'm not looking for the emotional story, just the facts. I start by sharing three major events from my life as an example—two bad and one good. I might say:

1. When I was 13 years old, my mother died.

2. In 1995, my first book came out.

3. In 2016, my younger son, David, died.

Those are the facts. There's no emotion and no story behind them. I only want the broadest strokes, bad and good. Then for the next round, I ask everyone to name the exact same three events, but this time, I want them to talk about the worst parts of each experience. I'll say, "Find something horrific or horrible about each of your moments," and someone will always say, "Wait. Even with the good one?" Yes, even with the good one.

In my case, I tell them:

1. When I was 13 years old, my mother died. It was so hard. I wasn't ready to be without a mother in the world. It was so lonely and isolating. I felt so different from my peers and classmates, and I didn't know how I would live without her.

2. In 1995, my first book came out. I wasn't ready for the public criticism.

3. In 2016, my younger son, David, died. It was brutal then and it's brutal at times still. There's no escaping that reality. The pain remains.

Those are my three stories told in the worst way. Can you guess what's coming next in this exercise? The three things never change. But now I ask people to talk about them in the best way and to mention something good about those experiences. People always ask, "Wait. Even with the bad ones?" Yes, even with the bad ones.

With my three examples, I'll say:

1. When I was 13 years old, my mother died. It was so hard. It changed the trajectory of my life and gave me this amazing career and a pathway to helping so many people manage grief in their own lives.

2. In 1995, my first book came out. I was officially a published author. Once an author, always an author. It's a great platform to have.

3. In 2016, my younger son, David, died. It was brutal. It has made me reach new levels in my compassion. I can now help people on a deeper level.

That's the exercise I want you to do right now. Let's start with just the facts. Without a story or angle, list three major events in your life, two good and one bad.

1. _____

2. _____

3. _____

Now, I want you to describe those events in the worst way. What were the negative parts of those experiences, the parts that made them especially difficult or painful? And, yes, even the good experiences have bad parts to them. You get a little more space to share your perspective here.

1. _____

_____

_____

2. _____

_____

_____

3. _____

_____

_____

Finally, reframe your stories once again, this time in a positive way. What were even the smallest good outcomes of each of those experiences, the parts that helped you grow or improve somehow? Maybe the bad ones made you more compassionate?

1. _____

_____

_____

2. _____

_____

_____

3. _____

_____

_____

When I do this exercise in my programs, I'll ask the group afterward why I had them tell three stories like this. People will usually say it's to point out that there's good and bad in everything. To find meaning, to view things from a different perspective, and to realize there's more than one way to see things. All those are accurate, but mainly it is to get people to become aware of the way they tell their stories. We all have different ways we tell our stories. How do you tell your story? Does your story change over time? I know mine did. For example, if you had met me in my twenties, you would hear the perspective of someone who had a victim mindset with intense abandonment issues. My mother left me, and I resented that for years. When I got a little older, I no longer wanted that to be my story. I wanted to fit in. Sure, I had bad things happen in my childhood, but who didn't? Other people experienced much worse things and greater traumas than I did, so I tried to minimize my loss. But at a certain point, I realized there was nothing to be gained from minimizing my experience. I began to see my story as a story of survival, resilience, and triumph.

This is how the mind works. Bad things happen, good things happen, and you can tell the story in a positive way or in a negative way, and everything in between. We've all met people who seem to find a silver lining no matter what bad thing occurs. The vacation gets canceled, the dog gets sick, the powers that be lay off the entire workforce, and some people will simply shrug and say, "What doesn't kill me makes me stronger." Someone else might tell you they overslept fifteen minutes and it wrecked their day. "And if that wasn't bad enough, the dog peed on the rug and then I had to throw away half a carton of sour milk." It might be that their grandfather died and the universe is out to get them.

How we tell our stories—to others and to ourselves—is how we navigate the world. What's important to remember from the last exercise is that the facts of the events do not change. How you tell your story is what makes the difference. You are not the author of the facts. I'm not the author of the story with the ability to retrospectively change the events of my mother dying, my book being published, or my son dying. But I am the author of how those stories get told. That's where I have some control, and where you have control too. Our mind holds all our memories. It holds the good ones. It holds the bad ones. How we choose to experience those memories is up to us.

It is healing for our stories to become broader and less rigid. Take a moment to reflect on your three stories and how it felt to shift the narrative in negative and positive ways. How does it feel to change perspective by thinking in a positive way about something negative, and a negative way about something positive?

_____

_____

The Trouble with Always and Never

What happens when the stories in our mind become rigid? Well, rigid thinking can quickly take a turn into binary thinking—when you start to see the world in terms of absolutes, like good versus bad, or right versus wrong. I see it happen frequently in my grief work. People will come into a session and insist that *nobody* understands them, that *everyone* is tired of hearing about their loss, that *everything* is different from how it used to be, and that *nothing* will ever feel right again. Sometimes I'll sit and listen. Especially if they're early in grief, I know it can feel like life has gone to extremes. *Everything* really does feel different.

But if I sense an opportunity for growth, I might counter a rigid statement with a gentle "Really?" As in, you really mean to tell me that there's not a person on earth who sees your pain? Because I certainly see it. Other people in the group see it too.

It may feel like self-protection to go to extremes with your thinking, but it's not always helpful. When people tell me how painful life is in the face of their loss, I listen to them to acknowledge and witness their grief, but I'm listening for "never," "always," and other extremes too. People will sometimes tell me, "This pain will never end" or "I will never be happy again." They might say, "I will always feel anger about what happened" or "This death will forever define me."

I'm curious whether this type of thinking resonates with you. Put a check mark next to the always and never statements below that you identify with:

☐ I will never be happy again.	☐ I can never love the way I once did.
☐ I can never forgive myself.	
☐ This loss will always create pain.	☐ I can never have faith in God again.
☐ Nobody will ever get my anguish.	☐ I will never find help for this pain.
☐ I will never get back to life.	☐ I will always be defined by my grief.
☐ I will always feel guilty about this death.	
☐ I will never learn to live with this loss.	☐ I will never find meaning from this loss.
☐ I will always feel alone.	☐ I never want to think about my loss.
☐ I will never join a support group.	☐ I can never move past this loss.
☐ I can never show my true feelings about my grief.	☐ I will never feel good again.

When I hear "never" and "always" from a person in grief, I understand why they are suffering so deeply, but it's important to remind them that their pain will not always be like this. Even with great despair, feelings change. I tell people, "I see this horrible, barely survivable pain you are in. But no feeling is final. Feelings will change." This is a message that the grieving need to hear, and in the moment of saying it, I often observe a shift. The person looks up and says, "It will?" And that person suddenly becomes lighter. When I do this with someone in front of an audience, people are shocked at the visible change they witness. Like I said earlier, pain from loss is inevitable, but suffering is optional. When the voice in someone's mind is whispering that they will always feel additional suffering, now I can interrupt that voice by offering the possibility of a way out, a different future—one more open to meaning.

Postcards to Your Past and Future Self

As long as you are alive, you have a future and the promise of release from your current pain. To prove this out, I'm going to ask you to do a variation on something else we often do at my programs. On the postcard below, I want you to write a note to your past. People often use this exercise as an opportunity to write something about a time when their loved one was still alive and what life has been like since. It doesn't need to be long. The point is to connect with who you were then from the perspective of who you are today.

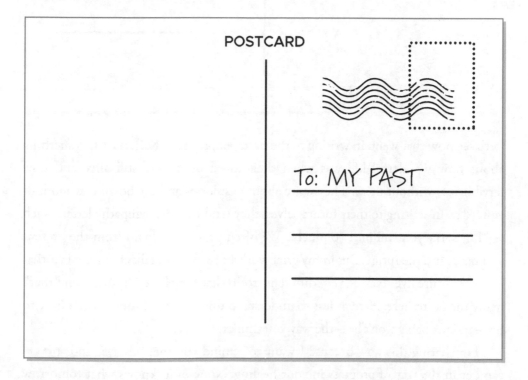

Now I'd like you to write a note to your future self. What would you say in a message to yourself in a time yet to come?

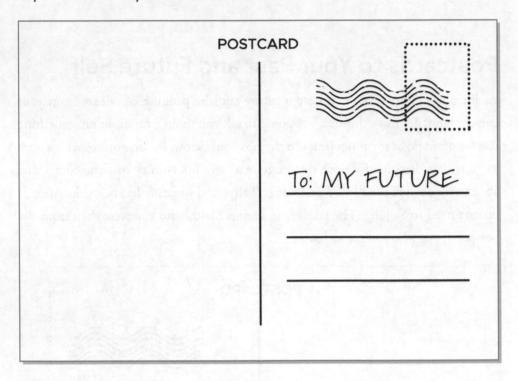

Let's see how that went. In writing to the past, people in grief often write something about how wonderful life was when their loved ones were still alive and how terrible it is without them. They write about past losses and the horrible wounds of yesterday. In writing to their future selves, they tend to write sympathy letters, such as "I'm sorry you still hurt so much." We often project our pain from the present and past onto the future. But in my grief workshops, we also talk about the fact that people's future lives may be very different from what they have imagined, and that's really the point here. Hard as it is to understand this now, the future doesn't have to be—and probably won't be—the way you think it will be.

I'm sharing this now because I want to remind you that "always" and "never" can get in the way of progress in your healing. None of us knows what tomorrow will bring, and I hope that as we move through these exercises, including the next powerful one, you'll stay open to new perspectives on your story and recognize that "always" and "never" might just mean "for now."

Finding Your Power

If you haven't figured it out yet, there's a larger intention built into these exercises. When someone's been taken from us, we sometimes feel not only that we've lost the person, but that we've lost control of our own lives too. When that happens, it's easy to feel powerless. I often talk about the three archetypes in grief: my lane, your lane, and God's (or the universe's) lane. Your power is always in your lane—in your behavior, in what you do, in what you believe. It's never what someone else is doing. It's never what "happens to us" by way of fortuitous or unfortunate events. Death robs us of power, at least at first; but then it's on us to reclaim our power and step toward healing.

These exercises help you do that. By helping you identify your feelings, they give you the power to say, "My grief is unique to me. What others think of my grief is none of my business." When old wounds come up—and old wounds will come up!—you can rely on these exercises to clear up distortions in the stories you carry about your grief. You can test these stories to see if they're true or not. For instance, if you see yourself as a "victim" in your mind, or if you say you'll "never" be happy again, or if you have unrealistic expectations of yourself or the people around you—you don't have to accept those ideas as fact. I'll say it again, the power is in your lane.

A colleague of mine was so upset because her mother made all the arrangements for a family member's funeral. The logistics came together very quickly and were done without any outside input—and certainly without consulting my friend. The result was that the memorial service was a grim affair with a handful of people. It was coordinated so quickly that out-of-town relatives were unable to attend, and the mood of the event was a complete mismatch for the happy, buoyant person who died.

The day after the funeral, I asked my colleague, "If you had the power, what would you have done differently?"

"Oh, first of all," she said, "I would have called it a celebration of life, not a memorial or funeral. And I would have allowed adequate time for all his friends and loved ones to make their travel plans so they could honor his memory in a way that fit who he was."

I said, "Well, why don't you do that?"

"Really?" she said.

"Yes, you do have that power."

"Wow, he would love that he got two events!"

Death robs us of many things, but it can't take away our actions, our decisions, or our best intentions. Obviously, we don't have the power to do everything we'd like. We can't bring a person back from the dead. We can't fix every situation that feels unfair or hurtful. We can't reverse time and change horrible events. But we can ask for what we want. We can be up front today about our feelings. We can strive to get our needs met by speaking truth to what's in our lane. Think about that as you answer the following prompts:

If I could use my power as I move toward healing, I would . . .

_____

_____

_____

_____

_____

_____

_____

What are some areas in your life where you feel powerful now?

_____

_____

_____

_____

_____

What are some areas in your life where you would like to feel more powerful?

_____

_____

_____

_____

_____

What could you do to feel more power in your life?

_____

_____

_____

_____

_____

Managing Grief Cues

Healing never follows a straight path. You may be doing okay and then suddenly you're feeling the massive weight of sadness all over again. It's as if the death happened just yesterday. Often, it's an outside cue or reminder that brings on heavy emotions. It can happen with a movie you're watching or a song you hear. It can happen when you pass a certain location or run into someone at a store or hear fireworks in the distance. Almost anything can instigate an intense grief wave. We often call them *triggers*. I try to call them *activators* or *intense emotional responses* when working with someone who has experienced gun violence or suicide, as using *triggers* here can be more harmful than helpful.

Interestingly, these heightened moments of emotion can be a roadmap to your grief. They tell you where the pain is but also show you where the healing resides. For instance, there's a park near my house where I used to go with my son. After David died, I was so fearful about the emotions that park would stir up that I avoided going anywhere near it. I would take other streets even if they were out of the way. I hated the reminder of how things were and would never be again. But then one day, I absentmindedly followed my GPS and drove right past the park. I noticed how much easier it was being there without all the emotional buildup.

When I didn't have anticipatory fear about the pain, the pain wasn't so bad.

Our minds want to avoid pain by geographically replacing it. We often do that with external cues. That movie will cause me pain. That street, that book, that hospital, and so on. If I avoid that cue, I'll never feel the pain, so I'll just avoid it. I'll never drive past the site of the accident. I'll never look on social media. I'll never listen to that song again. I'll avoid that room. I'll stay away from that grief group.

Here's something that might surprise you, though. If you take away those cues, the pain will still be there. That pain lives in you. The cues are just the reminders. It's not the schoolyard or the accident location that gives you pain. The pain is already there. When you're asleep, it's there. When you're on vacation, it's there. So, how can you feel those cues, allow them, and acknowledge them but also reframe them?

Not too far from the park, there's a street corner where I hugged David for the last time. That place is a grief cue for me. I avoided it for a while. I got angry whenever I went there before, but now I've reframed the experience. When I go there today, it's as if David is meeting me there. He's hugging me. It surfaces the memory of how sweet that hug was with him. Because I've reframed it, my mind can rest and live in the moment with the love I have for David.

Your cues are manageable even if they don't always feel that way. In this exercise, write down your grief cue alongside an idea or two for reframing your reaction. See my example as you get started.

What Is Your Grief Cue? (Person, Place, or Thing)	How Can You Reframe It?
Example: The street corner where I hugged David for the last time	Example: Imagining David is meeting me there, waiting with a big hug

Who Tells Your Story?

I hope you're seeing that the story of your loss can change by exploring it from different angles. That brings us to one of the most transformative exercises I know. As I've often recounted at my workshops and lectures, I've used storytelling to guide me through the grief work I've done over the death of my mother, and this exercise had the biggest impact on how the story of my mother's death changed for me.

As you may recall from *Finding Meaning*, my mother battled health problems throughout much of my childhood. On New Year's Eve 1972, I walked into her bedroom, gave her a kiss, and said, "Mom, 1973 will be the year you get better." Within days, she went into severe kidney failure and was transferred from our local hospital to one in New Orleans that was larger and better equipped. Mom was put in an intensive care unit that allowed visitors to see their family members for only ten minutes every two hours. My father and I spent most of our time sitting in the hospital lobby waiting for those brief, precious visits, hoping for a sign that she was getting better and could go home. Since my father had no money for a hotel, we ended up sleeping in the hospital waiting room and in the lobby of a hotel across the street.

That period in my life defined the words *confusion* and *chaos*. In *Finding Meaning*, I describe being in the hotel lobby when a man with a gun opened fire on the hotel roof, in what is now considered one of America's first mass shootings. During the two days that followed, my mother stopped talking and I knew she was getting sicker. But seeing her was a challenge since there was a rule that you had to be fourteen years old to visit a patient, and I was only thirteen.

Although most of the nurses were lenient and allowed me to go into her room, some wouldn't.

One nurse even told me to come back when I was fourteen!

Three days after the shooting, my father and I were told that my mom didn't have long to live, and unfortunately the next day it was the "Rule Nurse" who was on duty. She refused to let me see my mother or to ease up on the ten-minutes-every-two-hours regulation. Therefore, my mother died alone that day. That's the way things happened back then. Families, especially children, were often not allowed to be present during a patient's final moments.

When they were, it was only at the mercy of the caregivers.

The pain I felt from my mother's death lasted many years because there was so much unresolved anger and hurt complicating my grief. I told the story of that death many times over, always about how my loving mother abandoned me so young, leaving me all alone in the world. That simply reinforced my long-standing feelings of victimhood. But eventually I decided to consider it from a bold new angle. I sat down and wrote about her death in the voices of the other two people most central to the story: my parents.

I had always judged my father for how poorly he handled my grief, for not allowing room for my feelings, for leaving me to grieve in isolation. It was only years later, when I decided to write his side of the story, that I first imagined what it was like for him to lose his wife and become a single parent to a teenager. Instead of judgment, I found compassion for him. It was even more illuminating to write from my mother's point of view. She spent so much of her life in hospitals, including intensive care units, but I was never told much about what was happening. It was only by taking her perspective and writing about it that I first considered how frightened she must have been knowing she was dying and would soon leave her husband and only son behind.

The shift in the story also enabled me to understand for the first time that my mother hadn't abandoned me. My mother had died, but abandonment was how my young mind had interpreted it. When I retold the story through the eyes of my parents and realized how hard her sickness and death must have been for them, and how much they loved me and tried to protect me from being hurt, the new perspective became my freedom. I felt a deep gratitude to them.

I know this won't be easy, but I'd like you to shift the outlook on the story of your loss. Take a few minutes to tell the story you shared at the end of chapter 1, but now imagine it through the eyes of someone who saw it differently. It could be from the angle of the person who died, or another loved one. Maybe it's the doctor's view, or the EMT's, or someone else who was on the scene. Feel free to do this from multiple angles. The point is to tell the story from another person's voice and see how different it feels from the narrative inside your head.

_____

_____

_____

_____

_____

_____

_____

_____

_____

_____

_____

_____

_____

_____

_____

_____

_____

MEANINGFUL REFLECTION

Before we head into the next section, take some time to reflect on any insights you've discovered while exploring the story *behind* the story of your grief. Look back through your work in the workbook. Has your story changed? Broadened? Did any of these exercises unlock new ways of thinking? Were you able to find some self-compassion by telling your story in new ways or looking differently at the future? What changed by shifting the angle on the story you carry about your loss?

_____

_____

_____

_____

_____

_____

_____

_____

_____

_____

_____

PART 2

Moving Toward Meaning

The Sixth Stage of Grief
Acceptance and Beyond

> "We don't like loss. We will never be okay with it,
> but we must accept it, even in its brutality, and,
> in time, acknowledge the reality of it."
>
> —*Finding Meaning*

The work you're doing here cannot erase your pain. That pain is yours. It's part of the love you feel. But let me say again that if you are open to meaning, the pain will change, and the suffering will lessen.

By now you have gained some perspective on your pain and can look more honestly at your feelings; this next section requires the courage to go deeper. By surfacing the sticking points in grief, these next couple chapters zero in on what's standing in the way of acceptance and the meaning that lies beyond it. Which parts of your loss have you accepted and which parts haven't you? What feelings still need to be expressed, and how can pain transform into love as part of true healing that honors your loved one?

Acceptance is the first step in finding meaning. But it's not something you simply jump into. It grows slowly in us, and getting there can be brutal. In the first months after my son David's death, I stood over his grave and yelled, "Is this going to be the rest of my life, standing over your grave?" I turned to the skies in search of God and asked, "How could you let an accident like this happen?" I was traumatized, grief-stricken, and in a rage. In my mind, I fast-forwarded to images of years to come, picturing myself stuck forever in that moment, my son David still gone, my pain never-ending. I kept my gaze on the heavens, walking back and forth as I said, "Really, David? Really, God? This is going to be it?"

That is what acceptance looked like for me early on. I visited David's grave and I minimally accepted that he was dead. My limited acceptance was only because I saw his body go into the ground. Otherwise, I couldn't believe he was gone. But that early acceptance was also mixed with anger, and in my anger, I thought my pain would always be that enormous.

Today when I visit David's grave, the scene looks very different. You might see me clearing away some leaves or perhaps sitting there with the sun warming my face. But the anger and confusion are gone.

Acceptance isn't the end of grief. It is acknowledging the reality of the loss. You might find a little of it when you have a funeral or give away the person's clothes or turn their phone off. It's never easy to accept death, but how do we stop and breathe into the brutality of acceptance? That's what I'd like us to contemplate as we get into these next exercises.

A Different Type of Acceptance Speech

For this exercise, I want you to get clearer on what acceptance means to you. Perhaps you've already reached a level of acceptance around the death. If not, is acceptance something you're working toward? Is it something you're avoiding? Does the idea of acceptance bring you peace, or does it stir up fears around, say, losing your connection to the person? In my programs, I ask people to write down what parts of their loved ones' deaths they have accepted and what parts they haven't. Use the following prompts to explore that question as you write down the beliefs you have about acceptance.

The parts of this death I have accepted are . . .

_____

_____

_____

_____

_____

_____

_____

The parts I still cannot accept are . . .

_____

_____

_____

_____

_____

_____

_____

If I accept the death of my loved one, it means . . .

_____

_____

_____

_____

_____

_____

_____

_____

_____

_____

_____

_____

_____

Now examine what you wrote. Did you use the words *never* or *always*, as in, if I accept this death, I'm never going to be happy again or I'm always going to be in grief? Many people are afraid of acceptance because they think it means they'll lose the memory, and maybe even lose the love they have for the person. Did any of that come up for you?

If acceptance somehow equates to the loss of love or even to the end of grief, I want you to know that's not what happens with acceptance. Acceptance means you acknowledge loss. It doesn't mean you like it. It doesn't mean your pain is over. It definitely doesn't mean the love is over. Because the truth is, the love never dies, whether or not you accept the death.

Acceptance does not hurt or deny your connection. In many ways, it adds an important dimension to that connection. Acceptance is where we begin to make meaning after the person's death. It is in us. Meaning is what we make from their life. Meaning is part of the love. It is through acceptance of their death that we begin to ask the important question: "Is there something more to grief?"

Disloyalty Checkpoint

People sometimes fear that acceptance means being disloyal to their loved one's memory. If you catch yourself having a smile or a laugh or falling into a new routine, it can feel like you're allowing the loss or the grief to slip away somehow. You might not be fully aware that these feelings are present. A nagging sense of disloyalty can emerge on a subconscious level. But by identifying disloyalty as a thought pattern, you can start to see it for what it is: another dimension of your story that can keep you stuck in grief and slow your healing.

The point of this exercise is to check yourself for disloyalty. Imagine you've been stopped at a roadblock by the disloyalty checkers. The checkpoint agent is now shining a flashlight into the recesses of your mind to help free you from any places you're being disloyal. Put a check mark every time you answer yes to one of the agent's questions—and please be completely honest.

Do you ever feel disloyal when you . . .

- ❐ Find yourself laughing?
- ❐ Find yourself having fun?
- ❐ Are making a big decision?
- ❐ Are learning or trying something new?
- ❐ Do something for yourself?
- ❐ Make a new friend?
- ❐ Forget something about the person who died?
- ❐ Say goodbye to the person's clothes?
- ❐ Say yes to an invitation or experience?
- ❐ Change something your loved one liked?
- ❐ Think or talk about dating again?
- ❐ Change something about where you live?
- ❐ Skip a tradition or activity you shared together?
- ❐ Adjust your routine in some important way?
- ❐ Move?
- ❐ Have a few moments when you don't think of them?
- ❐ Forget a birthday, anniversary, or other milestone?
- ❐ Purchase something the person might have resisted?
- ❐ Pack up or give away the person's possessions?
- ❐ Go on vacation?
- ❐ Go on living?

Even if it's been years, my guess is that you said yes to a few of those questions. Feelings of disloyalty are hard to dislodge after someone dies. We have a sense that to live again is being disloyal. If your spouse died, would dating again be cheating? To grow would be a betrayal. Happiness would be treason. These thoughts can become your belief system and it sticks. As I wrote in *Finding Meaning*, much of this stems from the fact that, for most of us, there is no defined period of mourning. Back in the days when you wore black for a year, you knew that at the end of that year, you had given full due to your loss and could now throw off your "widow's weeds" (or the equivalent) and be given permission to reenter life. There was no sense that this would equate with disloyalty to the deceased. Whenever I hear someone who is concerned about disloyalty to a dead spouse, I gently tell them that their marriage vows were to last "till death do us part." The marriage contract ends at death. It is done. You honored your vows and completed your marriage contract. No one's vows include the afterlife.

Finding the Pure Grief Under the Disloyalty

Saying yes to a new place, a new activity, or a new relationship won't make us forget the person we're mourning. By accepting how we're changing and growing, it actually helps us connect with our pure grief. That is the love. We can honor the person's memory while we engage and show up in new ways in our own lives—as long as we can move past the self-judgment that locks us in place with feelings of guilt, sadness, and shame. Death ends a life but not our relationship, not our love, not our hope.

As a bereaved parent, I, too, have wrestled with the concept of disloyalty. After David's death, I only allowed myself to laugh after telling a funny story about him. A smile or a laugh felt okay if it was connected to him, but not otherwise. I don't remember exactly when it happened or what it was about, but at a certain point, I just laughed at something. I was startled, because it was the first time my laughter didn't relate to David, and I was immediately flooded with tears and self-judgment. What kind of parent was I to be able to laugh again when my son was dead? I could not have imagined that this was possible, and now that I'd done it, I didn't think it was right. I sat in that lost place for a while. Day by day, I had to beat down the belief that living again was a dishonor to my son who had died. I had to create a new image in my mind of what loyalty to David would look like. Loyalty would mean living a full life—not ever forgetting him, but putting his love into everything I did and everything I am.

What does loyalty look like to you in your grief? Are there new images of loyalty you would like to create?

_____

_____

_____

_____

_____

_____

The Life You Didn't Get

A woman whose husband received an early Alzheimer's diagnosis told me that she often felt robbed by the life she didn't get to have. She and her husband had married in their twenties, and after forty years together, she planned on a happy retirement with lots of travel and special time with the grandkids. "We were planning to go to Bora Bora, we were going to take dance lessons, we were going to have themed dinner parties," she said. "This isn't the life I signed up for."

The future you imagined is rarely the same when someone close to you dies. As a young kid, I thought my mother would live forever. I didn't plan on her being dead by the time I turned fourteen. I also expected, the way most parents do, that my two boys would outlive me. Standing at David's grave in the beginning, I would curse the fact that my "life plan" had gone awry and that I would forever be brokenhearted.

Our culture can become fixated on gratitude and appreciation for the things we have. The small wonders, the little blessings. But sometimes it's helpful to accept the things we're never going to get. Yes, I'm all for smelling the roses and thanking the universe, but it's okay to say sometimes, "You know what? I'm angry I don't get to see my daughter graduate from college. I'm sad I won't get to the South Pacific with my husband. I'm heartbroken my grandmother didn't survive to see our wedding."

To me, this is one of the best uses of this workbook. People in grief don't often get a chance to express themselves freely about why life (and death) are unfair. It can feel self-pitying to do it, and our friends or loved ones tend to steer us toward making peace with our lost dreams. They might say something like "Maybe you can go to Bora Bora with your sister instead" or "Grandma will be at the wedding in spirit." You can't blame supportive people for their kindness and their good intentions. The problem is they inadvertently minimize your painful feelings. They miss seeing you. But I want you to be seen, even if it is just for you. Use the following exercise to catalog some dashed hopes and sidelined dreams. It can bring you one step closer to accepting the reality of your loss.

In the space below, tell me about the life you don't get to have. Write down the trips you won't take together, the experiences that person will miss, and the moments you won't get to enjoy together. It may be painful to reflect on these now, but I promise, there's a practical reason I'm asking, as you'll discover later in the workbook. What are some things you won't get to do because of this death?

_____

_____

_____

_____

_____

_____

_____

Expressing the Unexpressed

When I ask people what parts of their loved ones' deaths they have accepted and what parts they haven't, my goal is not to judge their healing progress. Acceptance does not have a finality. The intention, rather, is to guide them to areas of their grief that have not yet been seen. The question leads them to the feelings that still need to be expressed. That is where their work and true healing lie—in those feelings. To help you in that discovery process, fill in the blanks after the prompts below.

If I truly accepted this death, one thing I would change would be _____

_____.

If I truly accepted this death, I would stop _____

_____.

If I truly accepted this death, my memories of my loved one would _____

_____.

If I truly accepted this death, I could finally _____

_____.

If I truly accepted this death, I would feel the freedom to _____

_____.

If I truly accepted this death, I would worry less about _____

_____.

If I truly accepted this death, I would tell _____ to

_____.

If I truly accepted this death, I would feel hopeful about _____

_____.

If I truly accepted this death, my future would be more _____

_____.

If I truly accepted this death, my connection to my loved one would _____

_____.

If I truly accepted this death, life would be different because _____

_____.

Notice what came up as you were doing that. Did you feel some freedom? More disloyalty? More sadness? Whatever it was, just know you are committed to moving through your feelings as they surface.

Acceptance Exercise

Acceptance can't happen if you are overwhelmed by self-judgment. I sometimes say judgment demands punishment. When you say, "I shouldn't still be feeling this grief," that's judgment. When you ask, "Why am I still feeling numb?" that's judgment. When you're reticent about accepting the death, that's judgment too. We often condemn ourselves in grief. No trial, no jury—just a verdict that we're the reason our loved one died. We killed them by not picking up the phone call or by not answering a text or by arguing with them the night they died. We punish ourselves for these normal activities. We didn't tell the doctor something. We didn't go to the nursing home. We were on vacation. We'd much rather judge our feelings than accept the reality of what happened. We'd rather blame ourselves than accept that reality.

That's because our brains want to find control. We do it through confabulation, or what some people call "honest lying." We believe our stories. We'll delve into confabulation in depth in the next chapter, but for now, know that our brains sometimes lie to us. We believe something is so true even when it's not. Even if we don't even test it. So often we convince ourselves that what happened before the death—the argument, the detail we forgot to share with the doctor, the fact that we fell asleep—caused the death. It doesn't matter that the true reason was something else—an illness, accident, overdose, and so on.

So how do we help ourselves? Many times, I'll tell people to picture the hurt you, the sad you, the scared you. I'll ask how old that person is inside your head. They'll often say that this person is ten years old, eight years old, maybe five years old. I'll say, *that's* who you're blaming. Imaging putting the weight of your blame, the weight of this responsibility, the weight of this punishment on that ten- or eight- or five-year-old. Does that sound fair? Does that feel kind? That child has no way out and we have to help them. We have to treat them with compassion and love. As you move toward acceptance and toward self-forgiveness, think with kindness about that vulnerable person inside you and how you would like that person to be treated. Thinking about your loss or losses, and about the self-judgment you may be experiencing, answer these two questions as an exercise in self-compassion.

What self-judgment about your grief do you need to forgive yourself for?

_____

_____

_____

_____

_____

_____

How would the kindest person you know tell you to do that?

_____

_____

_____

_____

_____

_____

_____

_____

I notice in my grief programs that people are sometimes surprised by the second part of this exercise. It can feel like a huge relief to view your innermost pain like a kinder, gentler person might. If you've been blaming yourself, you might use this exercise to realize that you're not the reason your parent died, you're not the reason your spouse died, you're not the reason your child died. With self-kindness, you begin to accept the reality of your situation, and that brings you a step closer to making meaning from your loss.

Grief Bursts and Love Bursts

When we move through pain and release it, we fear there will be nothing, but the truth is, when the pain is gone, we are connected only in love. In some ways, that's the miracle of acceptance. It is by working through the pain and letting it go that we arrive at the deepest place of connection to the person who died.

Though much of my work is about giving people permission to grieve fully after a loss, I also want to give them permission to keep loving. When I talk about remembering my son with love instead of pain, I recognize that love didn't stop with his death. His body died, but the love didn't. Look for the small seeds of love in the pain. Just like a delicate plant, we have to pay attention to it and nourish it. If we do, the love will flower once again in our hearts.

I often talk about grief bursts. Even though someone may think they've put the worst of their grief behind them, they have moments when, seemingly out of the blue, they burst into tears, overwhelmed with feelings of loss. These moments are all the more painful because they are so unexpected, and people are often caught off-balance by them. But there are comparable experiences that I call love bursts—those moments when suddenly, for no reason at all, we feel a surge of emotion for someone and tell them how much we love them. There will be times when you will suddenly well up with love for the person who died. You may feel that that love has nowhere to go because you can't hold your loved one, but the love continues. If you allow yourself to feel it, you will find great meaning. Death doesn't have the power to end your love.

Can you think of moments when you've experienced love bursts? I'd like you to write about it here. Love bursts can fill us up in ways that are profoundly nourishing. If you can't think of one immediately, I encourage you to recall a favorite memory of the person who died. Or maybe just an attribute. The way the person laughed. An unusual habit you had great affection for. It could be a sense memory—a particular smell or feeling. This exercise can be joyful, bittersweet, and deeply fulfilling. Drink in the memories and share in the following space a moment that captures your never-ending love.

No matter how long you were together with the person who died, it's not enough time, but the love you shared is not gone. It lives within you, as a part of you. On the most basic level, that is the definition of acceptance. Even without the person in our lives, our own lives continue. We continue to grow and change and experience new things, and none of that means we have forsaken or are being disloyal to our loved one. On the contrary, it is our love for them that gets us through the pain and helps us live with meaning. In the next chapter, we'll look at some of the ways complicated grief can slow our healing, and what to do when stigma or shame clouds the path forward. But for now, I'd like you to reflect on your overall insights from this chapter.

MEANINGFUL REFLECTION

What have you discovered while exploring your relationship with acceptance? We looked at some common sticking points that can keep you locked in your grief. Take a few minutes to consider what changed for you while doing these exercises. What surprised you about your sense of loyalty? Were you able to communicate feelings you haven't expressed before? Did you forgive yourself in some way? Are you any closer to acceptance?

_____

_____

_____

_____

_____

_____

_____

_____

_____

_____

_____

Working Through the Guilt

Making Things Right When
(You Feel) You've Done Wrong

> "Whatever the reason, when there's guilt,
> survivors will often punish themselves or
> attract people who will do it for them."
>
> —*Finding Meaning*

Five years ago, Lindsay's husband died by suicide. He had struggled throughout their marriage with depression and mania and was eventually diagnosed with bipolar disorder, but the treatment he received wasn't enough. He was unable to see any other way to find relief from the pain than death by suicide. Lindsay, who was a recent graduate of my grief educator program, shared openly with the group that guilt was among her strongest lingering emotions from the tragedy. She couldn't shake the feeling of worry or unrest you get when you think you've done something wrong.

"I feel guilty that I didn't show up for my husband in a way where he could talk to me about what was truly going on," she told us. "I also feel guilty that I wasn't paying enough attention about whether he was always taking his medication."

Before we dig into the work Lindsay and I did together to reframe her narrative, I want to share a few general thoughts about guilt and its powerful grip after someone dies. If there's one feeling I'd like people to examine around the death of their loved ones, it's guilt. And yet, guilt is probably the hardest of all emotions to undo. You wouldn't believe how often, and for how long, people blame themselves for not doing enough, for ignoring possible signs, or for taking step A when step B *might* have kept the person alive. It doesn't matter that illness and death are usually quite random and beyond our control. In the mind of someone who's grieving, there must be a specific reason for the death now and in that way—and often the most convenient reason is because of something the grieving person did or didn't do.

Unfortunately, ongoing guilt is almost never productive or useful in helping a person accept their grief and heal. Guilt is a way of punishing ourselves for errors or failures we believe we've made, and it locks us in a kind of prison of our own making. With guilt, we tend to be our own unforgiving judge and jury, and the bitter jailkeeper too.

In this workbook, we've been digging into the stories we tell about losses. Now I want to focus on how guilt shapes those narratives and share some useful techniques to help free yourself from what is almost always an unfair perspective on what really happened. Death is so big and out of your control that your mind would rather feel guilty than helpless. Take that in: *Your mind would almost always rather feel guilty than helpless.* It's how we make sense of the senseless. Something's wrong? Blame yourself.

But the truth is, guilt is a false means of stabilization. What we do with guilt after death is take knowledge from now, bring it back to what we didn't know then, and implicate ourselves: "I feel so guilty! I argued with them the day before they died" or "I didn't call them back the night they died." We all argue and disagree with people a lot. We've all had times where we didn't call someone back. What's different in these cases is, we didn't know at the time that the person was going to die the next day, that night, or that week. Guilt has a way of twisting the present to help us rearrange the past and distort things to place blame. We suffer as a result.

Guilt gives us a sense of power in grief—more power than we actually have. "If only I had kept a spreadsheet with my husband's medication schedule, he wouldn't be dead." But none of us has the power to stop death. If you did, you'd be on the front page of every newspaper and website in the world. Even in the movies, we can't stop death. One of my favorite movies is *Groundhog Day*. You might have seen it. Bill Murray plays Phil, a weatherman who keeps waking up in the same day again and again. The first day, a homeless man asks him for money. Phil says he doesn't have any. He sees later that the homeless man dies at the end of the day. Then, he relives the day. The homeless man asks him for money again. Now Phil realizes he's reliving the day without consequences, so he gives the homeless man all his money—yet the man still dies.

The third day, Phil decides to take things a step further. He gives the homeless man all his money, gives him food and water, and brings him inside out of the cold. The homeless man still dies. The next day, he says, "That's it." He gives the homeless man all his money, gets him food and water, brings him inside, and even takes him to the hospital. At the end of the day, the homeless man still dies. Phil can't understand it. He says to the doctor and nurse, "But I gave him all my money. I gave him food and water and I brought him inside, and even brought him here to the hospital." They tell him, "Sir, despite our best efforts, people still die in this world."

That scene has so much truth. Despite our best efforts, people still die in this world. You may be punishing yourself with the thought that you could have saved your loved one if only you'd woken up when you heard them making a noise, or if only you'd gotten them to their twelve-step meeting that day, or if only you hadn't been out of town the night the accident happened. The reality is, even if you'd woken up or gotten them to their meeting or stayed home from Hawaii, the person might still be dead. Or maybe you would have saved them that day, but they might have died the following week. As powerful as you are, you are not as powerful as the cancer, stroke, addiction, mental illness, or twist of fate that actually kills someone.

Someone in my group always asks at this point: What if we *are* the cause of death? Well, chances are, if someone truly and knowingly took a life, they are not coming to me to rid themselves of the guilt. But for the rest of us, it's worth examining that guilt. Usually, it's subtle. Guilt simmers in the background. We repeat its allegations but leave the need for evidence unattended. When you begin to think through guilt, you usually see that it doesn't hold up. So many times, I'll hear grieving parents say, "I shouldn't have let my child go play." Well, what was the alternative? Keeping the kid secluded in their room without friends or social contact? Sending them to the playground in bubble wrap? Or someone will tell me, "I should have insisted my daughter not ride that motorcycle" or "I should have urged my brother to stop drinking." That's when I'll ask them, "Did the person listen to every piece of advice you gave them before that day?" I'm sure not. Because our parents, our partners, our kids, our siblings, our friends—they usually do their own thing. If we tell someone not to do something, they often do it anyway. If we tell them to eat better or take their pills on time, they don't always do what they're supposed to do. When you really think about it, we don't have control over other people's lives. We certainly don't have control over their deaths.

The good news is, despite how much self-blame permeates the experience of grief, I've seen remarkable breakthroughs in how people understand and move beyond their guilt. In my grief programs, the burdens of guilt are often relieved by using the techniques I'm about to share in this chapter. This work isn't easy, and it will take time, but it's incredibly useful if your grief is defined, even in part, by self-accusation, self-condemnation, and self-punishment.

Four Techniques to Resolve Guilt

I. Confabulation Exercise

If you're early in your grief, I understand how hard it can be to recontextualize your feelings of guilt. This may not be the time for you to question what your heart is telling you. But with time, you may find it useful to examine your guilt through the lens of four techniques that have helped so many people I work with.

Let's take Lindsay as an example. For years, she was convinced that her husband's death by suicide was at least partially her fault. Even as she moved forward in her healing, even as she launched her own practice as a grief educator and a mentor to others facing loss, Lindsay was still gripped by the thought that she had not done enough to help her husband.

"What do you feel most guilty about?" I asked her.

"Not creating a safe space for him," she said.

When I asked for a specific example of what that meant, Lindsay recalled a conversation she once had in the car with her husband about starting a family. He was in graduate school at the time and Lindsay was working at a low-paying job, and she expressed her concern that they would never have enough money to support a child. "I put a lot of pressure on him," Lindsay said, "and that conversation was a microcosm of the larger pressures we were facing as a couple."

Lindsay saw the conversation as causation. I viewed it as confabulation.

Confabulation is the story we believe and are committed to—even when that story isn't entirely true. In grief, confabulation is the story we tell ourselves over and over. It becomes our rigid truth. Other possibilities can't be considered or even let in. My friend brought tortilla soup to her mother three days before she died in hospice of advanced cancer, and she forever blamed her mom's death on that tortilla soup. Hospice and very advanced cancer notwithstanding, the soup is what brought about her mother's demise. It's a fiction, but she deeply and rigidly believes it.

One sign that you're struggling with guilt is if you're burdened by what-ifs and if-onlys. Maybe you ruminate on mistakes, on decisions that came too late, on conversations you wish you had but never did. When we find ourselves thinking, "What if I had done things differently?" or "If only I had been there one day earlier," it's usually a signal that something needs to shift and that you are stuck in a cycle of self-blame. These what-ifs and if-onlys are almost always not true. Rather, they increase your self-doubt and put roadblocks between you and the person you want to become. That's not to say these regrets aren't useful. Bringing what you've learned from the past into the present and future is how you grow and find meaning. As I say in *Finding Meaning*, "The moves of the past have been played, but for the survivor, the future has many possibilities."

For the first exercise in this chapter, I want you to consider whether what-ifs and if-onlys are stopping you from moving forward in some ways. As I told Lindsay, people in grief sometimes hang on to questions about their own role in a death even if those questions aren't helpful or even reasonable. What if she hadn't made that comment to her husband about the cost of raising a child? What if she never talked to her husband about money? What if she had done more to make him feel safe in sharing his anxieties and pain? What if she had gotten him to a different psychiatrist or treatment program?

To see where you might be falsely accusing yourself, focus on the what-if and if-only questions that trouble you around the death of your loved one. It doesn't matter if you know deep down that the questions aren't useful; share them here.

What are the what-ifs or if-onlys in your grief story?

For example:

- If only I had not spoken with my husband about finances, he would be alive today.

- What if I had not asked for the morphine when my loved one said the pain was unbearable—would they still be alive?

- If only I had not brought in tortilla soup to the hospice, my mother would not have died.

What if / If only _____

_____

What if / If only _____

_____

What if / If only _____

_____

What if / If only _____

_____

Does anything stand out in these questions as inaccurate or faulty? Are you giving wisdom or future information that you didn't have at the time? Do any of the what-ifs or if-onlys feel unfair or self-incriminating in ways that don't line up with reality? If the answer is no, you might need to think deeper in the next step about what really caused the person to die. For now, I just want you to reflect on what these questions mean to you in telling your grief story. Why are you holding on to these what-if or if-only ideas?

_____

_____

_____

_____

_____

_____

_____

_____

II. Proximal Causation Exercise

Now we must look at other possibilities. This is a place to allow alternate stories in. As you consider other possible causes for your loved one's death, please keep your mind open. Think of this as your trial. I am your defending attorney. I want to build a case that you didn't cause the death.

To do so, I want to introduce the notion of *proximal causation*. This is a legal term, but I am using a different definition here. Our minds often think the event or thing we were doing closest to the time of death *must be the cause*. In other words, what happened right before the death caused the death. Our last interaction, the last phone call or text, even the tortilla soup—that must be the cause. This is the mind looking for patterns even when those patterns don't match up to true causation.

In the spaces below, write down your proximal causes—the reasons you have been blaming yourself for your loved one's death. Then, write down other possible causes for the death. You may not find these alternative explanations convincing, and that's okay; for now, simply identify what else *might* be true.

Cause 1

One thing I did (or didn't do) just before the death that I believe caused the death

is: _____

_____.

But another possibility is: _____

_____.

Cause 2

Another thing I did (or didn't do) just before the death that I believe caused the

death is: _____

_____.

But another possibility is: _____

_____.

Now that you have identified the proximal and other possible causes, it's time to put them to the test. The following techniques will help you evaluate how plausible each explanation truly is.

III. Scientific Method Exercise

When I was writing *Finding Meaning*, my editor kept pointing out that I always came back to this concept of what-ifs and if-onlys and self-judgment. She didn't want me to be repetitive, so she said, "I can fix this. Right up front, we'll have a sentence that says, 'Self-blame often accompanies grief but is not warranted.'"

I said, "That sounds great. But is it going to handle self-blame with people who are grieving?"

She said, "I don't know."

I said, "I do. It's not. That why I'm going to tackle what-ifs in a lot of different ways from a lot of different angles."

I often think about my time working in the hospital system and the patients who died in the emergency room from injuries sustained in car accidents. The nurses and doctors would inevitably ask the question "Was the person wearing a seatbelt?" We want to think that if the person died, they weren't wearing their seatbelt, and that if we wear our seatbelts, we'll be safe. You could see the disappointment on people's faces when they heard that someone wearing a seatbelt didn't survive.

As I looked at different ways to talk about self-blame in the book, it got me thinking about the scientific method. You may recall this from your fifth- or sixth-grade science class. For the results of an experiment to be accurate and true, that experiment must be repeatable and replicable—meaning that with the same setup, the experiment must produce the exact same results in different places to prove the findings are not random. For example, let's test the theory of gravity. If you drop this workbook to test gravity, it will fall to the ground where you are. If you were to test it again in ten different countries, you'd get the same results. It wouldn't even matter if *you* were the one dropping the book. A grandmother in Italy or a ten-year-old in

Australia could drop it, and the book would fall to the floor. Sir Isaac Newton was right. Gravity is reality.

But how can we test reality in our minds? In grief, we all have stories that give us some sense of control about what happened. To us, death can't be out of our control. The problem is we don't always take the broad view. Instead, we try to find something within our grasp that we can blame or point to as a cause. "If I hadn't told the hospice nurse to give the medication to my mother for pain, she never would have died." Someone else might say, "If I hadn't gone to lunch and was in the car with my husband, he wouldn't have gotten hit by the person running the red light and he would still be alive." Or "If they had gone to the ER sooner . . ." or "If they had taken an aspirin when they first felt chest pains . . ." or "If we hadn't had an argument that night . . ." The what-ifs and if-onlys are the bricks and mortar of the foundation we have built around grief guilt.

When I hear theories like those, I'll sometimes ask, "Do you know *for sure* that's how the person died?"

The other person will say, "Absolutely."

I'll say, "Okay, let's test it."

Then we'll apply the steps of the scientific method to reflect on the death of their loved one like a scientist would. Our goal is to see if their story is logical and supported by evidence. To see how this works in practice, let's test the theory about the pain medication morphine: *Do you believe if you hadn't asked the hospice nurse to give morphine for pain that your loved one would still be alive?*

i. Make an observation.

My loved one died because I asked the hospice nurse to give them the pain medication.

(Remember, we form a hypothesis to test this observation and see if it is true.)

ii. Form a hypothesis, or testable explanation.

Giving the pain medication kills people.

(Remember, we will test this hypothesis to see if it is true.)

iii. Make a prediction based on the hypothesis.

If giving pain medication generally kills people, the hypothesis is supported.

If giving pain medication does not generally kill people, the hypothesis is not supported.

iv. Test the prediction. Is it true (like gravity)?

If your prediction is true, it would mean morphine always kills. Does that hold up scientifically? You might think it must be true, but is it as consistent as this workbook falling everywhere in response to gravity around the globe? I once broke my arm and went to the emergency room, and they gave me pain medication—morphine. As far as I know, I'm still here and writing this workbook. The medication didn't kill me. They also give people pain medication, even morphine, in orthopedics wards and in labor and delivery. Those people usually don't die either. In fact, most of those delivery ward patients multiply. There's not more death, there's actually more life.

v. Form a conclusion.

It's *not* true that giving someone pain medication at the end of life kills them.

Let's use Lindsay's situation from the beginning of this chapter as another test case.

i. Make an observation (what she thinks, even if it is not true).

Lindsay's husband died by suicide because of their conversation about finances.

(Remember, we form a hypothesis to test this observation and see if it is true.)

ii. Form a hypothesis, or testable explanation.

Conversations about finances cause death by suicide.

(Remember, we will test this hypothesis to see if it is true.)

iii. Make a prediction based on the hypothesis.

If conversations about finances generally cause people to die by suicide, the hypothesis is supported.

If conversations about finances do not generally cause people to die by suicide, the hypothesis is not supported.

iv. Test the prediction. Is it true (like gravity)?

Think for a minute about all the conversations people have about finances, and use these results to test your prediction. Do financial conversations cause suicide? I have had many financial conversations. Some I didn't like. Some even caused me immense pressure, yet I didn't die by suicide, and my guess is that is just as true for you. So financial conversations don't consistently cause suicide.

v. Form a conclusion.

Financial conversations do not cause suicide.

Now that you've gotten a feel for how this exercise works, use the following spaces to test your hypothesis about the cause of your loved one's death using the scientific method.

i. Make an observation.

_____

_____

_____

ii. Form a hypothesis, or testable explanation.

_____

_____

_____

iii. Make a prediction based on the hypothesis.

_____

_____

_____

iv. Test the prediction. Is it true (like gravity)?

_____

_____

_____

_____

v. Form a conclusion.

_____

_____

_____

Did applying the scientific method help you clarify any errors in your thinking about the death of your loved one? Did forming a hypothesis and testing it change your theories about what really caused the person to die? Do your findings alleviate the guilt you've been carrying about your own role in the death? Use the space below to write about your insights with the scientific method.

_____

_____

_____

_____

_____

_____

IV. Occam's Razor Exercise

Remember: Your guilt is on trial. In defending you against your self-recrimination, we began with confabulation—the story you believe about your guilt whether it's true or not. Then we moved on to proximal causation, which says that our minds want to find a reason for everything—and often they decide the reason is our last action (or inaction) before the death took place. Think of it as the tortilla soup theory. We then used the scientific method to test the validity of that theory.

Now it is time to find the real reason. The science of self-blame is really the science of guilt. We need an answer for why our loved one died, and often the easiest answer is "It must be my fault." But that's usually not the simplest answer—or the truth. For that, I rely on the problem-solving principle from philosophy known as Occam's razor. First attributed to a fourteenth-century Franciscan friar and scholar from England named William of Ockham, Occam's razor is the belief that the simplest explanation tends to be the best and truest one. But it can be the elephant in the room.

If someone tells me they feel guilty that they asked the nurse for pain medication when their loved one was in hospice care, I'll ask, "Why was the person in hospice? Oh, they had advanced Stage IV cancer?" That's when I'll test the idea with Occam's razor. Once again, let's look at the facts: Pain management doesn't kill. Hospice doesn't either. Does advanced Stage IV aggressive cancer kill? Absolutely. So does addiction, accidents, mental illness, and severe heart failure. Those are the simplest and truest answers to why someone dies, no matter how much your mind tries to argue otherwise.

In Lindsay's case, you could ask, does severe, advanced aggressive mental illness cause suicide? Yes, it does. And as soon as you ask the question, it confirms that her husband's death had very little to do with Lindsay's actions and everything to do with the pain and suffering inside his head.

Too many what-ifs can be a sign that you're veering away from the truth of a situation. Part of my work is helping people understand the simple true reasons, not the complex ones, that are born of the what-ifs. Occam's razor helps us see that. Let's test the tortilla soup theory. My friend had spent weeks comforting her mother in hospice, where she was dying of end stage cancer. Three days before her mom died, my friend brought her tortilla soup, and afterward, my friend was convinced that it was the soup that had killed her. But how would that have worked? Was it the spices that were the culprit? Did the temperature of the soup do it? Was it the chicken? The tortillas? There are too many variables. It is much simpler to see that end stage cancer results in death.

You might ask, "What if I'd answered the phone when my brother called about needing a ride to a twelve-step meeting?" Not answering the phone or not giving a ride doesn't cause death, but advanced addiction does—that's the simple truth. Just like talking about finances didn't cause Lindsay's husband's suicide. His being mentally compromised did.

Think for a moment about how we miss the causes when we're not thinking about the reality of what happened. If we can assign blame to ourselves, maybe we can create the illusion that we can prevent another death in the future. But you have the ability to reshape your story in a more realistic way, and Occam's razor is the final step in doing that. Answer the questions below and let Occam's razor zero in on the truth of your loss.

My guilt says I caused my loved one's death because . . .

_____

_____

_____

_____

_____

_____

Occam's razor says they actually died because . . .

(Here you're looking for the simplest explanation—"the elephant in the room"— whether it be the accident, the illness, the mental illness, the addiction, and so on.)

_____

_____

_____

_____

_____

_____

We want to believe that if we do the right thing, we will get the right results. But as I hope I've made clear, sometimes we need to shift our thinking to get to the truth. Appropriately dosed pain medication doesn't kill, but advanced Stage IV cancer certainly does. Lindsay's husband died because of deep mental challenges, not because of their conversation about money. These are simple truths and also the most accurate accounts of what happened. The scientific method teaches us that we need to get results that are predictable and duplicatable. Applying Occam's razor helps us see simpler answers where once we saw only self-blame.

Now it's time to revisit the what-ifs and if-onlys from earlier in this chapter. For this exercise, I want you to recast your what-if statements as even-ifs. When you do that, you'll see that the person was still tragically going to die. Let me show you what I mean:

What-If	Even-If
If only I had not spoken with my husband about finances, he would be alive today.	~~If only~~ *Even if* I had not spoken with my husband about finances, he would ~~be alive today~~ *have died.*
What if I had not asked for the pain medication when my loved one said the pain was unbearable—would they still be alive?	~~What if~~ *Even if* I had not asked for the pain medication when my loved one said the pain was unbearable—~~would they still be alive?~~ *they would have still died, and in pain.*
If only I had not brought in tortilla soup to the hospice, my mother would not have died.	~~If only~~ *Even if* I had not brought in tortilla soup to the hospice, my mother would ~~not~~ *still* have died.

By thinking about the even-ifs, your what-ifs can lose the power and sway they hold. That happened to me. In the immediate aftermath of my mother's death, I often thought that I was to blame because I sometimes sneaked in salty snacks for her. She loved them and was always asking for them. For years, I asked myself, "What if I hadn't brought in those salty snacks? Would she still be alive?" But when I changed what-if to even-if, I knew that even if I hadn't brought her salty snacks, my mother's illness would have caused her death. In a way, I was giving myself too much power over her condition, and that wasn't fair to either of us. What I'm asking you to do now is to consider how your grief story might be unfair in some ways—and by that, I mean, unfair to you.

Even if _____

_____, my loved one would have died.

Even if _____

_____, my loved one would have died.

Even if _____

_____, my loved one would have died.

Even if _____

_____, my loved one would have died.

What-ifs and if-onlys keep us mired in the past with our grief. But by bringing what we've learned from the past into the present and carrying those insights into the future, we can turn regret and guilt into understanding and meaning. No matter what hand you've been dealt, it's futile to keep playing cards from the past. In the space below, take a few minutes to reflect on how turning what-ifs into even-ifs could bring some peace as you move forward in your experience with grief.

_____

_____

_____

_____

_____

_____

_____

_____

Take a moment to reflect on whether these four techniques helped change or resolve feelings of guilt you were holding around the death of your loved one. In what ways were you blaming yourself unfairly for the death? How might these techniques change your grief narrative going forward?

_____

_____

_____

_____

_____

_____

Now that we have explored the evidence against your self-blame, I rest my case. It is time for you to give your verdict.

Verdict of Your Trial

My loved one died because of _____.

(Note: If you still say that you are the cause, just know you can always appeal.)

As we conclude this chapter, I'd like to shift gears and share three of the most helpful exercises I know. Like the work we just did on guilt, these exercises are designed to spark meaningful changes with even the most difficult and stubborn emotions around loss. Meaning takes time, but these three exercises can help accelerate your healing journey if you allow yourself to be open to the process.

Installing the Good

In the last chapter, I gave you space to share some of the negative feelings about your loss. I asked you to catalog some things you won't get to do because of the death of someone close to you. Now I want you to do the opposite. I want you to appreciate the good. In times of sorrow and grief, this may require a proactive mind and creativity, but stick with me if you can.

As psychologist Rick Hanson says, "The brain is very good at learning from bad experiences, yet very, very bad at learning from good experiences. Neuroprocessing is privileged for negative stimuli. When a bad thing happens, we give more attention to the negative."

In other words, we are wired to *not* smell the roses. Negative moments, which are held in both short-term and long-term memory, become deeply wired and burned into our psyche. The same is not true for the positive ones, which are less likely to make it into the long-term memory bank. This is why you might forget positive moments with the person who died but the negative ones live in endless repetition. It's partly a survival mechanism. Events with bad outcomes are more urgent, so we remember them more than those with good outcomes.

Since we're so good at remembering the negative, how do we find good even in bad experiences and with difficult grief? Hanson teaches a technique called "installing the good" or sometimes "taking in the good." It helps us give more attention to the good, and I find it especially useful when someone's death has a person focused on negatives.

Installing the good involves three steps, which I invite you to try right now:

1. Identify a positive experience in your life now. Even if it is a small one. Hanson gives the example of thinking about how good your coffee tasted this morning. Positive experiences can also involve cuddling with your pet, savoring a dessert, taking in a sunset, enjoying a hug, or appreciating a conversation. You can do this with any experience, from the most ordinary to the most meaningful. Remember as many sensory details about the experience as you can—what you smelled, tasted, touched, heard, and saw, and how it felt.

2. Enrich it. Savor it. Think about it. Recall the moment again and try to hold it in your mind for twenty to thirty seconds or more. Recapture the good feeling in your body and in your emotions. Intensify it.

3. Absorb the experience. Sink into it and let it sink into you. Soak it in. Feel it in your body, visualize it in your mind, add music or a fragrance to recapture it, let it become part of you.

If you think there's no good to be found in your life anymore, identifying tiny good moments can be the beginning that changes everything. The coffee is still good. The sky is still blue.

Learning to live with loss is like any kind of learning. And learning to find the good, even in a small moment, as we are in pain is a particularly difficult kind of learning. I'm not suggesting you minimize or negate the pain, but if you only see pain in your life, nothing good can ever grow. By installing the good, you help find meaning in your life and take that good into the future.

Please reflect on what it was like installing the good.

_____

_____

_____

_____

_____

_____

Motivation Exercise

Once you work through your feelings, there will be a space left where the guilt was. We want to fill that up. We want to install the good there also. With that in mind, I'd like you to reflect on any guilt you feel around the death of a loved one. What specifically do you feel guilty about? And can you use that guilt as fuel, as motivation—even if only for the sake of this exercise—by focusing on what that guilt motivates you to do differently or to change in your life?

Here's the prompt, followed by a couple examples to show you what I mean. Please be compassionate with yourself as you think about your responses to this statement:

My guilt about _____ does not reflect the reason my loved one died. But it does motivate me to _____.

Examples:

- My guilt about not spending enough time with my mother at the end of her life does not reflect the reason she died. But it does motivate me to spend more time with people I love and care about in my life.

- My guilt about not stopping my daughter from riding her motorcycle does not reflect the reason she died. But it does motivate me to remember I don't always have control over what happens in the world.

- My guilt about not getting my father to the hospital earlier does not reflect the reason he died. But it does motivate me to eat better and exercise for my own heart health.

Now please fill in the blanks with your own examples:

My guilt about _____

_____ does not reflect the reason

my loved one died. But it does motivate me to _____

_____.

My guilt about _____

_____ does not reflect the reason

my loved one died. But it does motivate me to _____

_____.

My guilt about _____

_____ does not reflect the reason

my loved one died. But it does motivate me to _____

_____.

A Living Amends Contract

I'd like to share one more powerful exercise that can help people find meaning even in the most difficult, unshakable cases of grief. One of the most direct paths to meaning is to commit yourself to meaningful action with what I call a "living amends." As I've mentioned, guilt and what-ifs often color our view of what happened after someone dies. My hope is that this workbook has sharpened your ability to see how that type of thinking can be self-defeating and keeps you locked in grief. No matter what occurred, it's important not to confabulate or assign blame unfairly, particularly if you're blaming yourself for something beyond your control. Remember that missed phone calls don't cause death, but heart attacks do. Saying the wrong words doesn't kill someone, but drunk drivers do. The more you focus on the true cause, the less likely you will be to beat yourself up unnecessarily.

A living amends is where you take the action that you wish would have occurred during the person's lifetime and do it with others for the rest of your life. If you never told the person who died that you loved them, then you might say, "My living amends is whenever I love someone, I'll tell them. That will be my amends, my living, breathing apology." If, like Sally from my book *Finding Meaning*, you feel remorse or guilt for ignoring phone calls because of an argument and missed one last chance to speak with the person who died, you might say, "My living amends is that after an argument with anyone else, I will take their calls. This is my amends, my living, breathing apology."

If you brushed off a plea for help, if you stayed quiet about a case of addiction, if you said the wrong thing, a living amends gives you a chance at a corrective emotional experience. When you face your guilt and make a living amends, you can begin to fully grieve the person who died. Please review and sign the contract on the next page. You don't need a lawyer, just your best intention to do something meaningful in memory of the person who died. I've provided an example of my contract first.

Living Amends Contract

On this <u>12th</u> day of <u>September</u>, 20<u>24</u>, my living amends to the memory of <u>my son David</u> is to <u>enjoy the life and people around me now</u> as an apology for <u>all those moments I didn't enjoy life when he was around.</u>

This is my amends, my living, breathing apology.

Signed,

<u>David Kessler</u>

Now you give it a try.

Living Amends Contract

On this _____ day of _____, 20_____, my living

amends to the memory of _____ is to

_____

_____

as an apology for _____

_____

_____.

This is my amends, my living, breathing apology.

Signed,

_____

MEANINGFUL REFLECTION

In the section ahead, we'll take the work we've done to the next level. Having explored and excavated pain and tapped into your truest and most authentic feelings, you've gotten clearer about the story of your grief and how that story fits into your healing journey. In this chapter, you recognized where guilt may be holding you back, and how to see the truth in your loss where you once saw only self-blame. The next step is to use what you've discovered to bring more purpose to your life.

Before we move on, please reflect on any insights you gained in this chapter. Were the circumstances or feelings around the death of your loved one keeping you stuck in your grief? What shifted when you looked at the guilt you carry about your loss? Did you feel relief coming up with new ways to manage your emotions? What changes as you think about turning guilt or regret into action with a living amends?

_____

_____

_____

_____

_____

_____

_____

_____

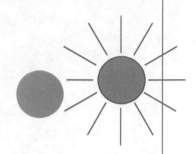

PART 3

Life After Death

5

Making Meaning

Identifying What Matters

> "No two people will react to an event in the
> same way. How you respond will depend
> upon the meaning you see in it."
>
> —*Finding Meaning*

Grief gives way to meaning even when that seems impossible. Consider the meaning that's been made from large-scale tragedies, such as 9/11. When bad things happen on a monumental level, people sometimes feel there is no point, or that the meaning must mirror the tragedy and occur on a grand scale somehow. But survivors make meaning. Those who join in moments of silence or participate in Heroes Runs each September make meaning. People who visit the 9/11 Memorial to remember, cry, and reflect—they all make meaning. Meaning is not found in the death but afterward, in us!

I heard about a California family that planted apple trees on their farm property each September 11 in those initial years after the tragedy. The family didn't know anyone personally who died that day, but they wanted to honor the memory of all those who perished and also pay tribute to the first responders who risked their lives. The planting ritual continued for ten years, but the meaning endures today. Many of those trees are now over twenty-five feet tall and collectively produce thousands of apples at the end of each summer. During the first two weeks of September every year, the family opens the orchard to the public so friends, neighbors, and visitors can enjoy the bright fruits of those trees, and at no cost. Most people filling their picking baskets don't remember that these apples began as a memory project. In a way, that doesn't matter. Apple picking makes people happy, the apples are delicious, and many new memories are being made in the process. The meaning is there because meaning is everywhere. Meaning can be found in the life of anyone who has ever occupied space on this planet or in someone's heart. It is there if you look for it.

Let me repeat that: *Meaning is there if you look for it.*

In *Finding Meaning*, I shared the story of my friend Linda, and I think it's worth repeating here since it has so much to offer. Linda was nine years old when her mother died of cancer. She felt robbed of a normal life and jealous of all the perfect mom-and-dad families that her classmates appeared to have. Not only did Linda live with the loss of her mother, but she carried a secret fear that the death of her father was always just around the corner. She would get very anxious whenever he went away on business trips, thinking it would be the last time she'd see him. Eventually she told her dad about her worries, and the next time he went away, he took Linda along. She was around twelve on that trip to Massachusetts. On their first night, after dinner, they decided to take a walk through the charming old city where they were staying. They came upon a small historic cemetery off one of the main streets and decided to explore it.

Linda noticed one of the headstones was engraved with the name and dates of someone who was born on March 15, 1802, and died on March 18, 1802. "This baby died after three days," she said to her father. "That's all he got, three days!"

For the first time, Linda thought about losses beyond her own, and she also realized how meaningful it was that she'd been able to share nine years with her mother when it could have been much, much less. Even with that sense of gratitude, she continued ruminating about her dad dying. He tried to reassure her that he would live for a long time, but Linda kept worrying. She told him she saw a commercial on TV for insurance that said, "What would you do if a loved one died and you didn't have the money to bury them?" Again, her dad tried to reassure her, but he saw the pain in her eyes and asked, "Would you feel better knowing I got one of those dollar-a-month policies?" And that's what he did.

Linda grew up and became a successful media professional. Her father lived into his mid-eighties. They were very close, and Linda gave her dad a beautiful send-off and buried him in the same cemetery as her mother. She was so grateful for the decades she had with her father that she all but forgot the anxiety she felt as a kid about losing him.

About six weeks after her dad died, Linda was at home getting ready for a cancer charity event that her TV network was sponsoring. She noticed a letter in the mail from Freedom Mutual Insurance and was stunned to find a check inside for $600. It was from the policy her dad bought after they saw the baby's tombstone. The irony didn't escape her that she no longer needed the money. But she wanted to find a way to use it in a way that honored her father.

At the event that night, Linda and her husband were chatting with colleagues when they heard the auction MC say the charity was just shy of the night's fundraising goal that would enable them to double the money. They were short by $600.

Without thinking twice, Linda raised her hand and offered the exact amount she received from her dad's policy. The charity reached their $500,000 goal, which meant another donor would double that to one million. The meaning in the moment gave Linda chills. A child who lived for three days in 1802 not only comforted her as an anxious twelve-year-old; now that connection would touch countless other lives through the cancer charity.

Like Linda, many people assume there is no meaning in loss. And sometimes we have to search long and hard for it or get help finding it. But it's there if we look. All of us get broken in some way. What matters is how we get the pieces back together again.

This final section of the workbook is about finding meaning even when you think meaning is beyond you. You've worked hard in these pages to excavate and examine the pain around your loss. You've identified what's true and what's inaccurate in the story of your loved one's death. Together, we've explored guilt, disloyalty, grief cues, complicated losses, the vast array of feelings that shape your emotional life, and what you can do to manage those feelings.

All that groundwork is important and useful, but you can't get to meaning unless you *decide* to get to meaning. I know that sometimes feels out of reach. It's easy to feel locked inside your pain. But as we've discovered, if you can start noticing small changes happening around you—sometimes despite yourself—you can push through resistance and discover meaning on the other side. To illustrate what I mean, we'll talk next about micro-moments of meaning: indicators so subtle you might not even recognize them as part of your forward momentum.

Indicators of Meaning

I often think about the words of my friend Dianne Gray, who once headed the Elisabeth Kübler-Ross Foundation and is a bereaved parent herself. In the early days after my son David died, Dianne saw how much pain I was in and said to me, "David, I know you're devastated. You'll keep sinking for a while, but there will come a point when you hit bottom. Then you'll have a decision to make. Do you stay there or push off and start to rise again?"

I knew she was right. I was still in the deep end of the ocean and wasn't ready to surface. But even then, by her just planting a seed, I became curious. Could I continue to live a meaningful life? I owed it to my surviving son, and to myself. I understood that I would need to go through all the stages of grief that Kübler-Ross described. But I also knew I couldn't stop at acceptance. There had to be something more.

People sometimes hear me tell that story and say, "Well, I'm still in the deep end of the ocean and I don't see a way out. I'm not continuing on with my life. I'm still down in the depths."

What I say to them is, life goes on. You're just not recognizing it. That's when I ask them to pay attention to the indicators of life. It starts with the most basic examples: Your heart is still beating—you can feel your pulse in your wrist.

You're still breathing. Your fingernails and toenails are growing. You can fight these indicators all you want, but if you're alive, those things are still happening. Acknowledged or unacknowledged, they are still going on.

Let's take a quick inventory based on where you are in your grief. If you are early in grief, circle all the indicators of life that apply to you in the first column. For those later in grief, circle the indicators of life in the second column. What I'm looking for are recent signs that you're still moving, still functioning, still on your journey, even in grief.

Early in Grief	Later in Grief
• You can feel your pulse.	• You laughed at a joke.
• Your heart is beating.	• You exercised.
• You are breathing.	• You're planning a trip.
• You felt hungry today.	• You attended a movie.
• You used the bathroom.	• You paid bills.
• Your fingernails are growing.	• You made a new friend.
• You moved your body.	• You did something creative.
• Your pet needs a walk.	• You tried something new.
• Your plants need watering.	• You met with a support group.
• The seasons are changing.	• You celebrated a milestone.
• Day becomes night.	• You signed up for a class.
• Night becomes day.	• You volunteered to help others.

I hope you get the idea. Even when we don't realize it, even when we fight it, even when we think meaning is impossible, life continues to move forward after a death. And when you acknowledge that, you're a step closer to recognizing the small, meaningful moments that happen all the time. People sometimes hear me talk about "making meaning" after someone dies and assume I mean doing something big, like starting a foundation, naming a 5K after your mom, or committing to a yearslong cause. But meaning does not need to involve such grandiose efforts. Most of us won't find large-scale meaning. That's okay. Meaning more typically comes from personal change: Returning to your place of worship. Taking up a hobby you've wanted to pursue. Going to the gym, visiting a spa, taking a vacation. Meaning starts with a tiny whisper from within that says *yes*.

A man once told me he could find no meaning after his wife died in a boating accident. He spent two hours convincing me that the tragic loss could never have meaning. He simply missed his wife and wanted her back. I listened and I understood. But I also asked if he might consider that meaning sometimes happens on a micro level. It had been a year and a half since his wife's death, and I asked if any part of her lived on in him—a habit she helped create, a change she inspired, a new way of seeing.

He smiled a little—it was the first hint of a positive emotion I'd seen in his face all afternoon—and said, "You mean the 25 percent rule?"

"What's that?" I asked.

He explained that since his wife's death, almost every time he eats at a restaurant, he tips 25 percent because his wife used to tease him about being a not-too-great tipper. "I can almost hear her voice every time I leave extra money for the waiter," he said.

"Do you think that's meaningful?" I asked.

"I think it is meaningful for the server, definitely," he said. "And it makes me feel better too, I guess. I'm doing something my wife would smile over."

So, what's your version of the 25 percent rule? Is there something small you do that brings meaning *because of* the death of your loved one? A positive change in your behavior? A meaningful new habit? A regular small tribute of some kind? What's a small thing you do because of your loved one's death that brings you meaning in some way? Think about a change their death has inspired, a habit they helped create, or a trait that lives on in you or improves the world in some way. Please share any changes that come to mind in the space below.

_____

_____

_____

_____

_____

_____

Small Steps Journal

Let's take this a step further—in fact, one step closer to finding meaning. You may remember the woman I describe in *Finding Meaning* who posted on my Facebook page that it had been four painful years since her son died and she hadn't been able to find help. It's a case of old trauma. She said she couldn't find help as a kid when she was in pain, and she couldn't find help now. I asked if she was simply sharing her experience or actually looking for help.

She responded with, "The pain is unbearable, nothing will help."

I asked where she lived. I was afraid she might live in a small town with few resources. But she told me she lived in a major city. I sent her a link to Grief.com and told her there were some free support groups in her area.

She wrote back to say, "I'm not a group person."

I told her I understood and sent her a link to some counselors in her area.

She responded, "I can't go out."

"Are you physically challenged?" I asked.

"No, the grief is just too much to bear."

"You never leave the house?"

"Just for work, groceries, and sometimes Starbucks."

"I have an online workshop and group that may help you," I told her.

"I can't afford to pay for it."

I explained that I was happy to let her attend for free if she couldn't afford it. She agreed, and I asked for her email.

"I don't give out my email address. I don't like giving out identifying information."

I thought to myself, "Isn't that what an email is for? So we don't have to give out identifying information?"

But I also saw what was happening. There was nothing I could do to change her mind. I had done everything in my power, but I couldn't force help on her. Many people, because of trauma and old wounds, are unable to get the help they need because they don't feel like there's anything they can do about their suffering. The reality is, there is something everyone can do. Small steps are what's needed.

It's hard to not feel stuck in pain and grief at times. I see us always between stability and change. Death throws us to the extreme of change. The extreme of change is chaos. The extreme of stability is stuck. But your life continues on even when you don't think it can, even when you don't want it to continue. If you don't know how to move forward, I want you to know that you can make big changes by making very small changes first. When you're unsure of what to do next, often the best thing to do is to take small steps. As a griever, after months or maybe even years of wondering how anything can be meaningful after the loss you experienced, you may gradually start to notice that you are deciding to live again by noticing incremental changes, which are those small steps I'm talking about.

As I write in the book, these subtle shifts tend to show up when you least expect them. You may not suddenly plan vacations or go to parties, but you might be shocked to discover that you still enjoy the taste of a great espresso, or that you want to take a long walk in the park with your best friend. Little by little you begin caring about things, both large and small. The sheer momentum of life moves you forward.

For this exercise, I'd like you to pay closer attention to the small steps you're taking. In my grief groups online, I'll sometimes ask attendees to put notes in the comments about steps they've taken recently—things that surprised them, things that showed them their lives are continuing. Here are some of the things they wrote during a recent gathering:

• Read a travel magazine	• Felt good in an outfit
• Listened to music again	• Cooked a new recipe
• Went to a movie theater	• Talked about something silly
• Stayed out late with friends	• Complimented someone
• Finished a really good book	• Enjoyed a new restaurant
• Took a yoga class	• Shared a funny meme
• Volunteered for a good cause	• Did something nice for myself
• Noticed a pretty bird in my garden	• Asked someone about themselves

None of these are big-deal activities on their own, but taken together, they give you hope—at least they give me hope—that healing is possible. Taking small steps toward healing doesn't mean grief is over or that the person has forgotten about their loss. But each of these incremental changes feels like a win, a kernel of promise, an intimation that meaning is possible. Eventually, these wins become gratitude.

I'll sometimes ask people to keep a record for a week of small activities that give them hope. But for this exercise, I'd like you to write down your small steps toward meaning. What are the little pleasures and small positive moments you've noticed recently? Try not to overthink it. Maybe you caught yourself humming a song. Maybe you noticed unusual clouds outside your window. Perhaps you enjoyed a delicious meal. Big things, small things, it doesn't really matter. The point is to list as many small steps as possible:

_____

_____

_____

_____

_____

_____

_____

_____

What we pay attention to grows. Like breadcrumbs, little steps may lead to something greater than yourself. Take one more moment to reflect on what the small steps you're noticing mean to you. Are they leading you someplace unexpected?

_____

_____

_____

_____

_____

Subtraction and Addition

It's one thing to be a detective for meaning in your life. Now I'd like you to go beyond merely noticing meaning—and to start making it.

You may recall from *Finding Meaning* that six months after David's death, our sweet old dog, Angel, died. One year later, we decided to get a puppy. I was hyperaware that I was choosing another adorable dog to love and that the odds were good that she would be leaving us too, in about fifteen years at most. In the midst of my painful forced separation from my son David and our dog, Angel, I was choosing to attach again, even though I knew it would result in loss. I didn't need to get a dog again, but I purposely made a decision to bring love and new life back into our home. There had been so much subtraction, it seemed time for some addition.

People are surprised to hear that grief is optional. If I wanted a life without grief, I could have it. But that would mean no children, no partner, no friends, no pets, no love, no attachments. Avoiding the prospect of love also means avoiding the joys of life. In his book *The Problem of Pain*, C. S. Lewis wrote, "Try to exclude the possibility of suffering which the order of nature and the existence of free wills involve, and you find that you have excluded life itself."

After David died, I saw life continuing around me. I saw my hair and fingernails grow. My heart was still beating. I decided that it must be for a reason, and that I should make a conscious decision to live, not just be alive. Writing *Finding Meaning* was part of my conscious decision to return to life. So was my work with thousands of people dealing with grief in their own lives. This workbook is part of that decision to live again too.

You already know what has been subtracted from your life. We've taken time here to reflect on that loss in all its magnitude. Now I'd like you to think about addition. I am not suggesting you get a puppy (unless you want one!). This is another place to start small. I'd like you to consider adding something new to your life that doesn't relate to your loss or loved one. Perhaps try a new restaurant. Or go to a movie in a neighborhood you've never visited. Maybe it's walking in a different area or asking someone from your bereavement group out for coffee. People in my grief groups now travel together. Use the space below to list ten potential additions as a nod to making meaning. Small things are fine, and so are bigger things. It might be booking a two-week trip or just going on an afternoon outing somewhere. The point is to think about various ways that meaning adds up.

These are ten meaningful additions I could make in my life:

1. _____

2. _____

3. _____

4. _____

5. _____

6. _____

7. _____

8. _____

9. _____

10. _____

To me, addition is hope. It doesn't mean you forget the person. They are unforgettable. It certainly doesn't mean you're "moving on." What it says is that you're choosing to live in a way that honors the person you loved, while also committing to something meaningful in your own life. Before we go deeper and discover new pathways to meaning, take another look at your list of additions and use this space to reflect on how it feels to see life continuing even in the midst of your grief.

_____

_____

Your Loss Inventory

We've been talking so much about losses around death. But grief isn't always about someone dying. Grief and loss can be about any change that happens. I believe that loss is the change we didn't want. Many times, we don't even realize it, but an empty nest is a loss, getting laid off is a loss, a friend relocating to another city is a loss. Making a list of all the losses you've been through is a way to visualize the changes you've experienced. But above all, it shows the courage you have, the mountains you have climbed, and the resilience you have found. Looking at your losses helps you see your gains.

I use the loss inventory exercise in my Grief Educator Certification program I run. It's interesting because when I sat down to compile my own loss inventory, I thought I knew what would be on there. My parents, my son, various friends, pets. But since I knew that loss extended beyond physical death, I ended up with a list of losses that almost surprised me in how much they mattered. Here's what I came up with:

Name: *David Kessler*   Birth date: *February 16, 1959*

1. *1969: Home destroyed*

2. *1973: Mother died*

3. 1976: Moved out west

4. 1981: First breakup

5. 1982: Dropped out of college

6. 1985: First job loss

7. 1987: Father died

8. 2011: Nephew Jeffrey died

9. 2016: Son David died

10. 2017: Pet dog Angel died

Notice how many shapes and faces loss has. These moments are transformative and have a massive toll on our emotions, our behavior, our relationships, and our direction. The list I made doesn't contain every loss I've experienced, but it represents the big ones that changed me the most. Now it's your turn. Write your own loss inventory. In chronological order, list the ten biggest losses that you've experienced in your lifetime. (I recommend doing this in pencil because you often have to move things around.)

Name: _____ Birth date: _____

1. _____

2. _____

3. _____

4. _____

5. _____

6. _____

7. _____

8. _____

9. _____

10. _____

Seeing a list of losses can be quite confronting and even depressing at first. Look how much pain and suffering you've endured! But I truly believe that facing a list like this is an exercise in perspective taking and growth. When you can gain perspective on your loss, you can make meaning from your loss.

To me, a loss inventory is a step-by-step account of your hero's journey in grief. I'm sure you know the concept of the hero's journey, even if you don't think you do. The hero's journey is a common plot found in many stories and across different cultures. It's the basis of almost every big Hollywood movie you've ever seen, whether it's *The Wizard of Oz*, *Star Wars*, *The Matrix*, *The Lord of the Rings*, *Moana*, or *Barbie*.

The Hero's Journey

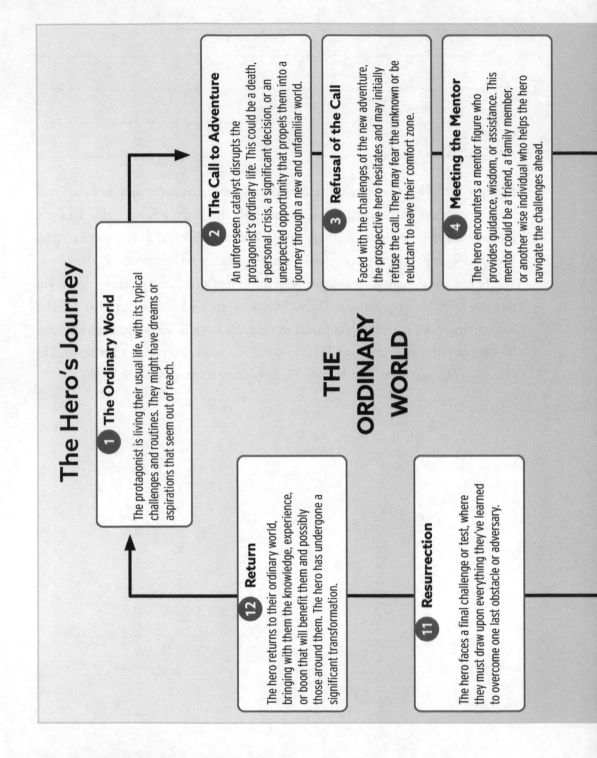

1 The Ordinary World

The protagonist is living their usual life, with its typical challenges and routines. They might have dreams or aspirations that seem out of reach.

2 The Call to Adventure

An unforeseen catalyst disrupts the protagonist's ordinary life. This could be a death, a personal crisis, a significant decision, or an unexpected opportunity that propels them into a journey through a new and unfamiliar world.

3 Refusal of the Call

Faced with the challenges of the new adventure, the prospective hero hesitates and may initially refuse the call. They may fear the unknown or be reluctant to leave their comfort zone.

4 Meeting the Mentor

The hero encounters a mentor figure who provides guidance, wisdom, or assistance. This mentor could be a friend, a family member, or another wise individual who helps the hero navigate the challenges ahead.

THE ORDINARY WORLD

12 Return

The hero returns to their ordinary world, bringing with them the knowledge, experience, or boon that will benefit them and possibly those around them. The hero has undergone a significant transformation.

11 Resurrection

The hero faces a final challenge or test, where they must draw upon everything they've learned to overcome one last obstacle or adversary.

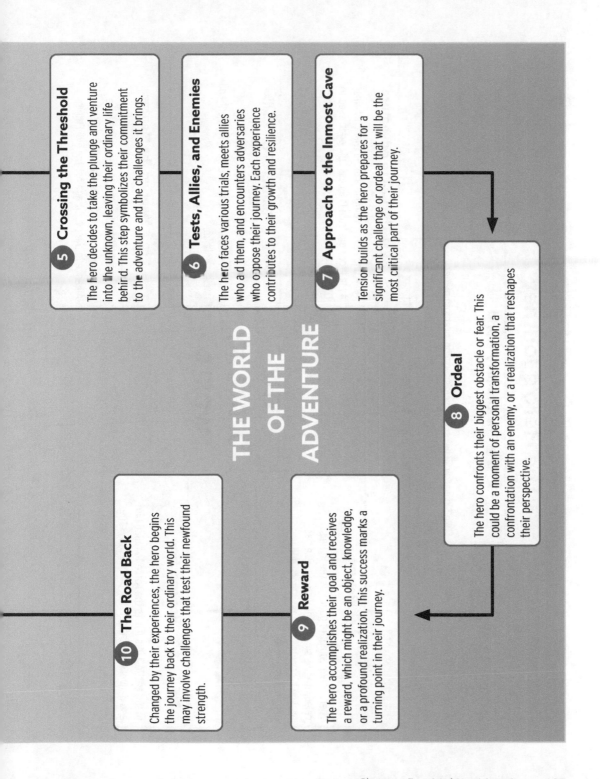

5 Crossing the Threshold

The hero decides to take the plunge and venture into the unknown, leaving their ordinary life behind. This step symbolizes their commitment to the adventure and the challenges it brings.

6 Tests, Allies, and Enemies

The hero faces various trials, meets allies who aid them, and encounters adversaries who oppose their journey. Each experience contributes to their growth and resilience.

7 Approach to the Inmost Cave

Tension builds as the hero prepares for a significant challenge or ordeal that will be the most critical part of their journey.

THE WORLD
OF THE
ADVENTURE

8 Ordeal

The hero confronts their biggest obstacle or fear. This could be a moment of personal transformation, a confrontation with an enemy, or a realization that reshapes their perspective.

10 The Road Back

Changed by their experiences, the hero begins the journey back to their ordinary world. This may involve challenges that test their newfound strength.

9 Reward

The hero accomplishes their goal and receives a reward, which might be an object, knowledge, or a profound realization. This success marks a turning point in their journey.

The Hero's Journey

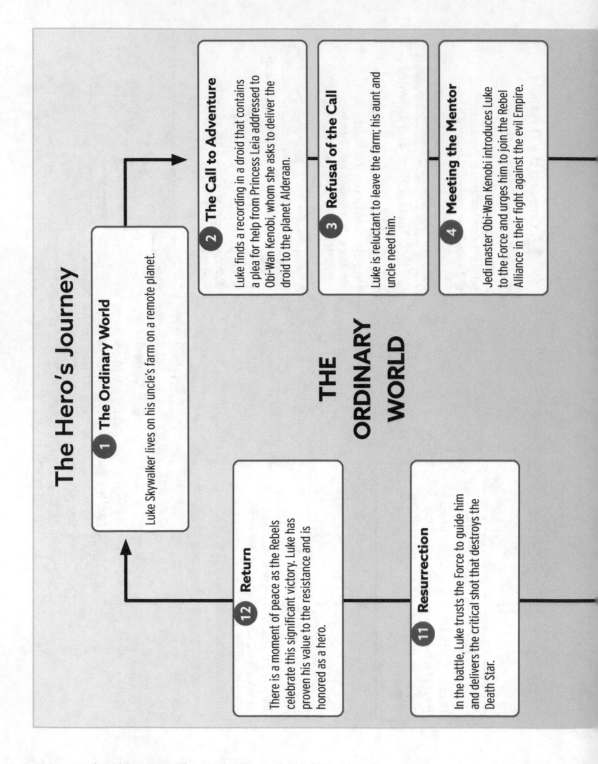

1 The Ordinary World

Luke Skywalker lives on his uncle's farm on a remote planet.

2 The Call to Adventure

Luke finds a recording in a droid that contains a plea for help from Princess Leia addressed to Obi-Wan Kenobi, whom she asks to deliver the droid to the planet Alderaan.

3 Refusal of the Call

Luke is reluctant to leave the farm; his aunt and uncle need him.

4 Meeting the Mentor

Jedi master Obi-Wan Kenobi introduces Luke to the Force and urges him to join the Rebel Alliance in their fight against the evil Empire.

THE ORDINARY WORLD

12 Return

There is a moment of peace as the Rebels celebrate this significant victory. Luke has proven his value to the resistance and is honored as a hero.

11 Resurrection

In the battle, Luke trusts the Force to guide him and delivers the critical shot that destroys the Death Star.

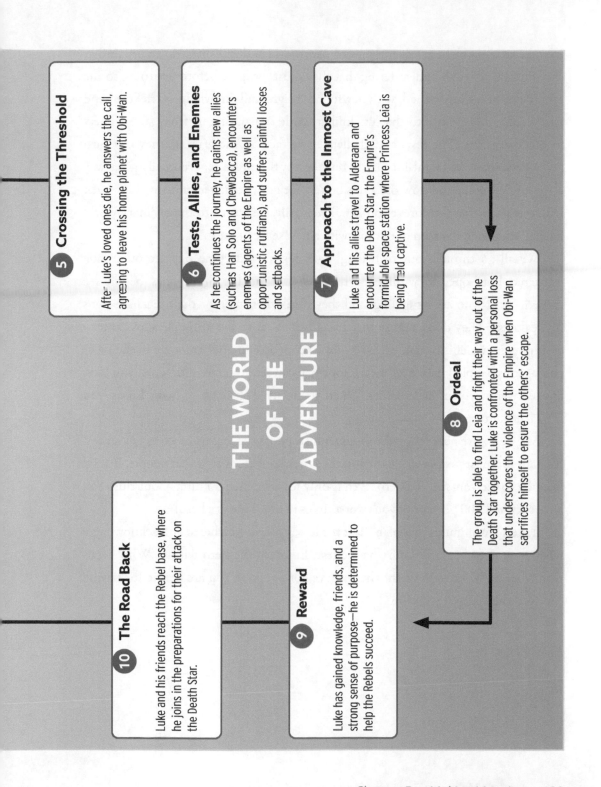

5 Crossing the Threshold

After Luke's loved ones die, he answers the call, agreeing to leave his home planet with Obi-Wan.

6 Tests, Allies, and Enemies

As he continues the journey, he gains new allies (such as Han Solo and Chewbacca), encounters enemies (agents of the Empire as well as opportunistic ruffians), and suffers painful losses and setbacks.

7 Approach to the Inmost Cave

Luke and his allies travel to Alderaan and encounter the Death Star, the Empire's formidable space station where Princess Leia is being held captive.

THE WORLD OF THE ADVENTURE

8 Ordeal

The group is able to find Leia and fight their way out of the Death Star together. Luke is confronted with a personal loss that underscores the violence of the Empire when Obi-Wan sacrifices himself to ensure the others' escape.

10 The Road Back

Luke and his friends reach the Rebel base, where he joins in the preparations for their attack on the Death Star.

9 Reward

Luke has gained knowledge, friends, and a strong sense of purpose—he is determined to help the Rebels succeed.

In these stories, the hero leaves their ordinary world and is thrust into an unfamiliar situation full of trials and suffering that they must navigate before returning to the everyday world transformed, with newfound insight and knowledge. Grief can send us over the threshold into that unfamiliar world, separating us from all we knew in our daily lives. The tests and challenges we face on the grief journey can turn order into chaos and light into dark. But the abyss, I promise, eventually gives way to peace. We come to know ourselves better. We grow stronger in many ways, even with our parts that feel forever broken. Eventually, we return to the ordinary world having integrated the pain of our loss with a new sense of meaning.

We all go through our own long, dark nights and come out the other side impacted, but hopefully willing and ready to continue life. Sometimes, people see those in grief who are struggling, and they think their pain or their tears are signs of weakness. They don't realize the strength it takes to live through a loss and to continue on. Grief is brutal, which is why I say people in grief are some of the most courageous people I have ever met. I hope you can see your strength when you look at the inventory you made earlier. When you've lived through so many losses, you are a true hero.

Maybe you've never thought about your story of grief as part of a heroic journey. It's hard for most people to see themselves as heroes; heroes are other people. But I'd like you to see yourself as a hero, even if only for a moment. Think about this: You have survived 100 percent of your worst times in life. That is a hero!

Take a few minutes to look back at the losses you've weathered and acknowledge what a survivor you are. Don't be modest. Embrace the hero within. Who needs Iron Man or Wonder Woman when you've got . . . you? You are heroic for having survived the losses in your life.

If you're still having trouble believing this, I invite you to consider the following diagram. It shows the phases of the classic hero's journey again, this time overlaid with a real-life experience of grief. You'll also find a blank template where you can reflect on your own grief journey. This should be a space for exploration; your experiences do not need to fit perfectly into the outline. Even in fiction, the hero often reaches the phases of the journey in a different order, or they may venture forth in entirely new directions. Each hero's journey—including your own—is unique.

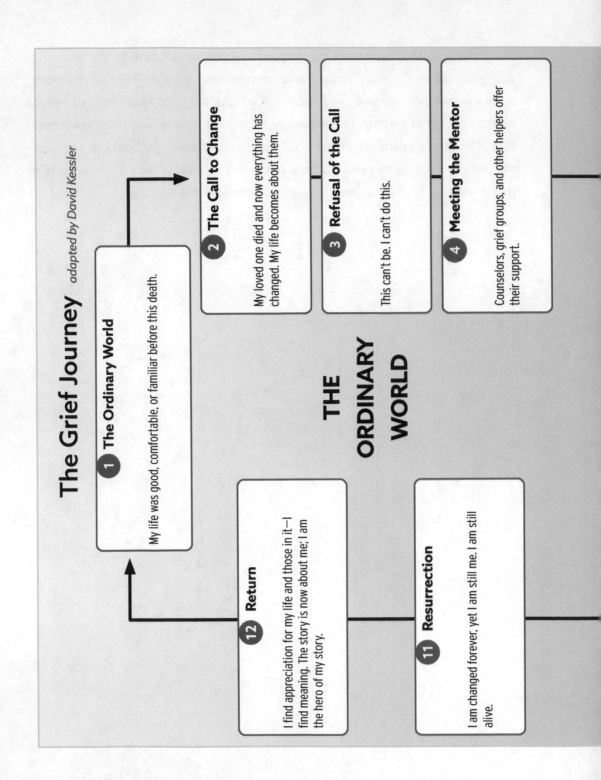

The Grief Journey *adapted by David Kessler*

1 The Ordinary World

My life was good, comfortable, or familiar before this death.

2 The Call to Change

My loved one died and now everything has changed. My life becomes about them.

3 Refusal of the Call

This can't be. I can't do this.

4 Meeting the Mentor

Counselors, grief groups, and other helpers offer their support.

THE ORDINARY WORLD

12 Return

I find appreciation for my life and those in it—I find meaning. The story is now about me; I am the hero of my story.

11 Resurrection

I am changed forever, yet I am still me. I am still alive.

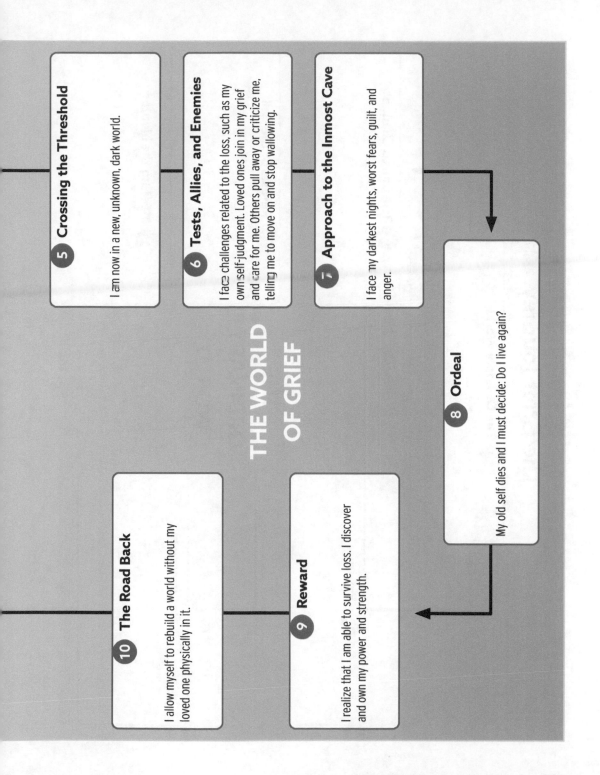

THE WORLD OF GRIEF

5 Crossing the Threshold

I am now in a new, unknown, dark world.

6 Tests, Allies, and Enemies

I face challenges related to the loss, such as my own self-judgment. Loved ones join in my grief and care for me. Others pull away or criticize me, telling me to move on and stop wallowing.

7 Approach to the Inmost Cave

I face my darkest nights, worst fears, guilt, and anger.

8 Ordeal

My old self dies and I must decide: Do I live again?

9 Reward

I realize that I am able to survive loss. I discover and own my power and strength.

10 The Road Back

I allow myself to rebuild a world without my loved one physically in it.

The Grief Journey *adapted by David Kessler*

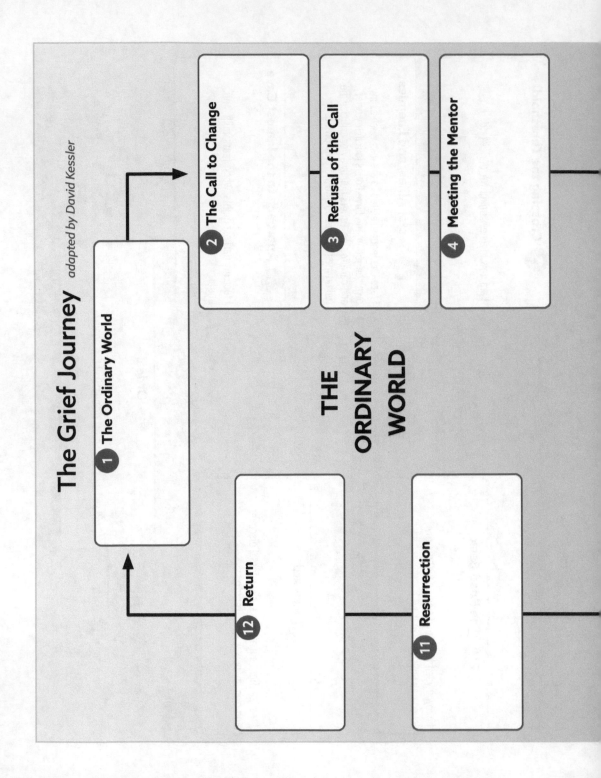

1 The Ordinary World

2 The Call to Change

3 Refusal of the Call

4 Meeting the Mentor

THE ORDINARY WORLD

12 Return

11 Resurrection

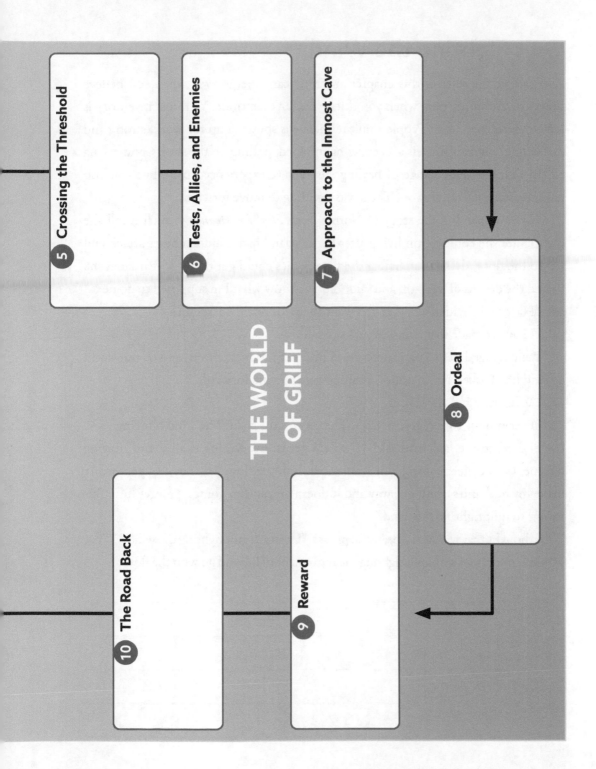

THE WORLD OF GRIEF

5 Crossing the Threshold

6 Tests, Allies, and Enemies

7 Approach to the Inmost Cave

8 Ordeal

9 Reward

10 The Road Back

Quit Fighting the Wind

As I said at the start of this chapter, meaning can emerge even when you believe there's no meaning, even when you think you can't continue. Your loss inventory is really a resilience story. People think resilience is showing up for work, strong and not crying. But resilience is also crawling into bed, pulling up the sheets, and crying all day. That is the courage of healing. Yes, you've experienced pain, but you also have the strength to carry on. The key is deciding to move forward.

If you remember the story of Norma from *Finding Meaning*, you'll recall she wasn't sure she could go on living after her husband had a sudden heart attack and fell to the floor, dying even before the paramedics could get there. A year later, she shared the depths of her pain and said, "I don't know what I'm supposed to do next."

"Have you decided whether you want to live or not?" I asked her.

"I haven't made that decision yet," she said.

I encouraged her to pay attention to her body, to her actions, and to the world around her. I asked her to notice if things were moving forward.

"What things?" she asked.

"Everything. Your digestive tract. The cars on the road. The wind blowing."

She called me later and said, "David, I get it. Everything is alive and moving but me. I can collect cobwebs, or I can move with the flow. My moving again won't make my husband's death go away and it doesn't mean I'm going to forget him. But I want to quit fighting the wind."

I thought that was such a beautiful phrase. "I want to quit fighting the wind." What would it mean to you to quit fighting the movement of life and go with the flow?

_____

_____

_____

_____

Letting Go and Moving Forward

Through meaning, we can transform our pain. By finding purpose, our grief becomes something rich and fulfilling. As we end this chapter, I have two brief exercises that can help clear the way to meaning so you can make major shifts and lasting change.

The first is a little like organizing your stuff before a big move. A friend of mine is a professional organizer, and she strongly encourages her clients to let go of household items that aren't serving them. Tools they've never used, gifts they're keeping out of guilt, compact discs cluttering up the garage. "Let it go, let it go," she tells them.

Here, I'd like you to attempt the same thing, except with emotional possessions rather than the physical kind. What parts of your emotional life do you want to leave behind on your path to finding meaning? For me, at a certain point, it was bitterness, anger, and turmoil. I felt those psychological states were keeping me from living a life of meaning. In the next chapter, we'll do a follow-up to this exercise and consider what you'd like to take with you from the loss. (I'll explain that in the pages ahead.) But for now, based on where you are in your grief, what are the things, emotionally speaking, that you'd like to box up and get rid of? My organizer friend gives her clients a checklist, so I'll give you one too. Mark the items you'd like to let go of on the checklist on the next page.

☐ Anger	☐ Irritability
☐ Helplessness	☐ Resentment
☐ Guilt	☐ Self-judgment
☐ Loneliness	☐ Other: _____
☐ Rage	☐ Other: _____
☐ Fear	☐ Other: _____
☐ Melancholy	☐ Other: _____

Checking those difficult emotions on a list doesn't magically dissolve them, but it does set an intention. As I'll show you in the next chapter, who you are now in grief isn't the person you will always be in grief. That brings me to the second exercise. I hope after the work in this chapter that you're seeing how grief changes with time. That's because grief changes you. You don't stop developing and growing after someone dies. As long as you are alive, you are moving forward and evolving. So, here's my question: How are you transforming and changing in grief?

_____

_____

_____

_____

_____

_____

MEANINGFUL REFLECTION

In the next and final chapter, we're going to push beyond small steps and modest additions and start mapping a future that's full of meaning. Before we do, I'd like you to reflect on what surfaced for you as you began to identify and track meaningful moments. Did anything surprise you in this chapter? Was it hard to think in terms of "addition" after all the subtraction you've experienced? What did it mean to reframe your grief and loss as part of a hero's journey? Reflect on the sense of hope—even glimmers—you felt when you noticed yourself taking small steps toward healing. Finally, please share any positive emotions you feel as you let go and move forward on your path toward healing.

_____

_____

_____

_____

_____

_____

_____

_____

_____

_____

Mapping the Future

Picturing a Life of Meaning After Loss

> "After sitting at countless deathbeds,
> I can tell you, no one pines for their
> houses or cars at the end of life.
> What is meaningful is the people
> whom they have loved."
>
> —*Finding Meaning*

Grief never ends, but the pain does change as you navigate your way toward meaning. If you're alive in this world, the quest for meaning is an ongoing part of your story. Meaning is how you grow and move forward, and it is ultimately how you honor the love and the loss of your loved one. When you aspire toward meaning, you pay tribute to the person's life, their death, their love, and the time you shared together on this journey.

As we approach the end of this workbook, I hope with all my heart that you've found these exercises useful in framing and identifying what you're feeling around your grief, and in taking important steps toward healing. For me, the shortest path I know to healing is meaning. Creating purpose in your life, acknowledging that your time here on earth matters, finding opportunities to help and give to others, using your grief as a catalyst for growth and change—those are the most powerful ways to transform your pain and live more fully.

This last chapter of the workbook is designed to shift your focus from intention to action and offer ideas on moving ahead on your path. Meaning doesn't always come from changing what's around you. It's changing yourself that makes the biggest difference. In these remaining pages, I want to share with you the strategies and principles that work most effectively in building new habits of mind.

I understand that change might have once seemed impossible. After a loved one dies, it is natural to feel frozen in pain and in grief. But you've answered the call by doing this work. No, you cannot go back to the way things were before the person died. Life goes on and you are forever changed. The world around you still may not get all the loss and pain you've suffered, but life does continue. If you ride the horse in the direction it's going, if you say yes to new things, if you recognize little accomplishments, you really can change. Remember, life changed without your permission, so you have permission to change. These closing exercises are meant to inspire and offer hope as we zero in on making yourself grow around the grief instead of making that grief smaller. As we get into this work, I encourage you to take note of your wins and let life lead you someplace.

Progress Report: Your "I Can" List

When people first come to one of my online grief groups, I'll typically ask them, early on, how they feel on a scale from 1 to 10, with 1 being "the best" and 10 being "the worst."

Often, I'll hear, "I'm a 10." "I'm a 15." "I'm 1,000!"

They can barely talk. They're crying through the whole sentence.

After, say, six months, I'll notice they're better able to express what is in their hearts and describe their feelings. They look much more grounded. They're not crying quite so much.

And so, I'll ask them again, "How do you feel?"

Just as often, I'll hear, "I'm a 10." "I'm a 15." "I'm 1,000!"

The point is, in grief, we tend to feel like we're always on the most painful edge of our feelings. When assessing our emotional state, particularly when we're facing loss, we speak from the worst pain of the day. But we miss something meaningful when we do that; we don't acknowledge the progress we've made. Healing is always about progress, not perfection.

Take this workbook, as one example. Think about where you were, emotionally, when you started versus where you are now. It's unlikely you are in the exact same place you were when you sat down to do the first exercises. Let's take a moment to recognize the ground you've gained, not just with this work but with your pain in general.

Here's what I'd like you to consider. What are some activities or ways of thinking that have changed for you since the earliest days of your grief? I know this isn't easy, but I want you to think about the growth and improvement you've made. Phrase your progress in the form of "I can" sentences. Examples might include:

- I can get through an hour without crying.

- I can get through a day without crying.

- I can laugh again.

- I can be present with family members.

- I can focus more at work.

- I can enjoy a night out with friends.

- I can enjoy a meal.

- I can tell a story.

These changes might feel modest, but please try to identify and articulate them. What are five "I can" statements that show your progress?

I can _____.

I can _____.

I can _____.

I can _____.

I can _____.

What to Do with Meaning?

Two years after her brother died from complications related to early onset Alzheimer's disease, a woman named Zelda contacted me to say *Finding Meaning* had inspired her to make room for meaning in her own life. Enough time had passed, she said, for her to "step out of the story of my grief and consider how my brother's death could be a teacher for me." I appreciate how she phrased that. Loss is not a "lesson," but you can definitely learn from it. It gives you clues on what you valued before the person's death and what you value now. Loss can show you what you need more of, what's truly important to you, and how you might help others.

In Zelda's case, she wanted to honor her brother's life and spirit by taking action in some new way. Meaning can come from doing. So, she began bringing her guitar to the memory care center, where her brother spent his final months, to sing and play for the residents. Zelda had played guitar in her twenties but put it aside after she went to work at her job in marketing. Now she was playing the old songs she loved and also learning new ones from books and YouTube videos. Even if the residents at the memory care center couldn't always express themselves with words, she could tell from their eyes that they appreciated her music. One day, a nurse at that facility asked Zelda if she would play at a senior center where the nurse worked part time, and Zelda became a regular there too. She also started teaching guitar to adults who wanted to learn or get back into playing like she did. "My brother loved music, and I think he would have been proud of me for picking up the hobby again and sharing it with others," Zelda told me. "Now whenever I'm playing guitar, I feel my brother is cheering me on."

I love how Zelda turned loss into meaning, and it was all because of love. When someone we love dies, that loss—and that love—has an amazing power to transform us. As devastating and painful as that event is, it can also connect you with people, nurture your creativity, and add movement to your life. Zelda took the music inside her that connected her to her brother and put it into the world. It might be your loved one's talent that connects to yours. Or their generosity or kindness. Look around and listen when people talk about why they do things. You will often find meaning connected to a loved one there.

Now that we've explored the pain of your loss and worked hard to understand the authentic story of your grief, you've seen that meaning surfaces in big and small ways, even when you're not looking for it. Here, I want you to look further into the meaning of your loss. Please respond to the following questions to clarify what you've learned from your loved one, and the meaning you're discovering.

If your loved one could see through your eyes, what would you be proud to show them about your life today? For example:

- I am more compassionate now.

- I'm more determined to make the world a better place.

- I explore new places.

- I am doing new things.

- I've taken up a new hobby.

- I've gone back to an activity I care about.

- I keep my loved one alive by telling stories.

_____

_____

_____

What do you value more since the death of your loved one? For example:

- Life itself

- Time with others

- The gift of time

- New connections I'm making

_____

_____

_____

What are some ways you feel you are growing or changing for the better? For example:

- I've become more loving.

- I've become more caring.

- I've become more appreciative.

_____

_____

_____

How is your love for the person who died making you a better person today? For example:

- I help others who are new to grieving.
- I feel more deeply.
- I am more compassionate with myself.
- I am more compassionate toward others.

_____

_____

_____

It's true that helping heals. How might you help someone else, with love and loss as your guide? For example:

- When people in grief tell me what they are going through, I help by sharing my experience.
- I just listen to others in grief without trying to fix them.

_____

_____

_____

Mapping Your Saint Nikolai

Near the end of *Finding Meaning*, I talk about the time I gave a lecture in Hamburg, Germany, and how surprised I was that everything there looked relatively new. I expect cities in Europe to be old. Even though I knew about World War II and

Hitler and had visited the concentration camps at Auschwitz and Birkenau, the explanation for Hamburg's contemporary look surprised me.

"The British and Americans bombed it in World War II," I was told, "and the city was destroyed, so it had to be rebuilt from scratch."

I was embarrassed I didn't know that history, and I made a point to visit the only part of the city that had not been torn down and rebuilt—the church of Saint Nikolai in the center of the city, which had been left standing in ruins exactly as it was the day after the bombing. It endures as a memorial to those who were killed during the air raids. Today, a peace garden and sculpture are monuments to the universal longing for peace and reconciliation. Even with the blackened remains of the beautiful bell tower shrouded in sadness, the ruins of Saint Nikolai seemed to be a testimonial to continuity and resilience.

You may remember from the book that I met with a volunteer there named Helga, who told me she was five when she watched her parents run from the fires to try to save her. Helga saw flames from above engulfing her mother and father, and everywhere she ran, there was nothing but the fiery red of the flames. Someone yelled at her to look for the dark spots, the only places where there was no fire. But then that person, too, vanished into the flames. Helga ran from dark spot to dark spot and somehow survived.

I was quiet after she told the story. Coming from a country that dropped the bombs that killed her parents, as well as tens of thousands of others, all I could say in response was, "I'm so sorry."

"I used to be angry," Helga said. "But as I matured, I understood that it had to happen that way for the good of the world."

What a remarkable woman. She was able to see beyond the viewpoint of a child and recognize the terrible history that explained what happened to her parents. She was now a citizen of the world and had assumed the responsibilities of citizenship, where she saw herself as part of something larger.

I often think about Saint Nikolai Church, forever destroyed, sitting in the middle of a beautiful modern city, how it sits there still in ruins. Yet transformation often occurs in the ruins. I think of my dear sweet son David. There is a part of me that stands just like Saint Nikolai, my heart forever devastated by his death. I know the pain and longing will never go away until the day we are reunited. Yet I feel like Hamburg. I've had to rebuild around the devastation.

Your heart may be devastated. You may feel destroyed. You may feel like your loved one was the only thing that gave you meaning. But I hope you've discovered here that meaning lives within you and is always possible to find again. You can continue to connect meaningfully with those who are still living and form new connections too. Those connections do not diminish your love for the person who died. They will only enhance it.

Just like in Hamburg after the war, we must be architects of our lives after loss. David would not want his death to constrict my life. He would want me to expand with his memory and love, and that's what I try to do every day. We like to believe our grief will grow smaller in time, but it doesn't. We must grow bigger.

For this next exercise, I want you to visualize what this looks like in your life. I know part of you stands like Saint Nikolai, forever destroyed. But how are you also like Hamburg, building and growing around the devastation? On the map on the next page, your loss—your Saint Nikolai—is that shaded-in spot near the center. The other open sections are yours to fill with names, activities, or perhaps drawings or symbols that represent the ways in which you are rebuilding. I'm imagining one spot on the map might include an exercise or meditation practice you've started, or it might mention a grief group you're attending. Another might have the name of a new friend you've made. Another might have a picture of a beach destination you're hoping to get to next summer. Think of this map as a picture of your resilience. Remember, your grief never goes away. It's always going to be near the center of who you are. But you're also never going to stop growing and living and discovering. I can't wait to see what you come up with.

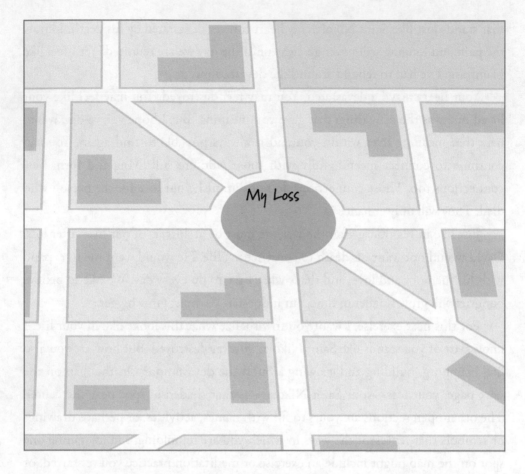

Here are some examples of new things in my life that have emerged on my life map since David's death:

- New friend Liz Hernandez

- New friend Will Reeve

- New dog Lucy

- New online grief group

- My older son's marriage

- Trip to Yosemite National Park

- New Grief Educator Certificate Program

Living Their Love

In 2015, I was asked by one of my publishers to write short bits of grief support for a card deck. My first reaction was resistance. I was used to writing books, not card decks. Then I thought of how many people shared with me that they had "grief brain" and could only absorb a little bit at a time. Now I see how helpful these short-form thought bites are in my *Healing Grief* card deck. As one of the cards, I wrote:

> *Remember your past, cherish your memories. Don't live only*
> *there. You are still alive, look around yourself today. See the new*
> *day. You are still making memories. There is more of life to come.*
>
> *Trust the process.*

There is a process in each one of us that moves us toward trust. Of course, we are human and wonder if healing is possible. It is—if we allow the love we have for the person to lead the way.

Love lives on ever after a person dies. Love lives on inside you. How will you nurture that? When you remember how someone loved you, and you embody that love, you are honoring their life and memory. When you direct that love toward yourself, you bring meaning to everything you do.

In grief we are faced with the question of how we will find meaning in the rest of our lives. Though we cannot help thinking that what would be most meaningful would be to have our loved ones back, we know that is not possible. Faced with the reality that we didn't get enough time together, we must ask ourselves, "What would best honor the years they didn't get?" That could be one way of bringing meaning to our lives without them.

People often think there is no way to heal from severe loss. I believe that is not true. You heal when you can remember those who have died with more love than pain, when you find a way to create meaning in your own life in a way that will honor theirs. You are healing fully when their loss doesn't fully control you. Their love impacts you more than the way they died. It requires a decision and a desire to do this, but finding meaning is not extraordinary. It's ordinary. It happens all the time, all over the world.

Thinking about the words above and about the ordinary decision and desire to find meaning, I'd like you to reflect with more love than pain on the person who died. Remember how they loved you and how you loved them, and think about what it would mean to love yourself like that.

Spend a few minutes writing about what it would mean to love yourself in the name of the person who died—in their honor, in their memory. What does it mean to love yourself as you loved them and they loved you?

_____

_____

_____

_____

_____

_____

_____

_____

The Chapters of Your Life

Remember how I mentioned earlier that storytelling can guide you in your grief work and healing? We become the stories we tell ourselves. That's why I asked you to tell the story of your loss and to consider that story from different angles as a way to test the story to make sure it's true.

Something I didn't mention is that when we're in grief, we tend to be inside our loved ones' stories. The chapters of their lives become our chapters. One chapter might have been their diagnosis or their accident or the phone call. Another, their illness or final moments. Another, their death or their funeral. It may feel like your loved one's story was the only thing that gave your life meaning. But, as I said, meaning lives within you and is always possible to find again. It might seem like all meaning slipped away in the chapter in which the person died. But in my experience, the ultimate meaning is in everyone you loved, including the person who died. Your loved one's story is tragically over. For unknown reasons, their time on earth has drawn to a close, but *yours continues*. I can only invite you to be curious about the rest of the story of your life. A crucial part of the work of healing is to understand the pain of their story ending and to realize your attention now needs to move to your story and your chapters.

I encourage you to begin thinking about the way your story is changing, and how your life still has chapters yet to be written. I sometimes imagine an afterlife where, in some form, I will see my parents again, my nephew, and all those who have died before me. Mostly I hope to see my dear son David again. He may know everything that happened in my life since he died. But perhaps not. Maybe he and my mother and others will ask about the time I received after their deaths. I know if I told them I spent the last thirty years of my life grieving them, it would break their hearts. They would tell me how life was a gift. What did I do with that gift after them? What's my story? Did I make the last chapters of my life meaningful? I certainly hope I have something to tell them. I want them to be touched by my grief and proud of the life I live in full after them that honors them.

I hope this is true for you too. In the space that follows, I'd like you to assign titles to the chapters of your life since your loved one died. "Life" might be first chapter. Then "Death." The "Beginning of Grief" might be another chapter. But what else is there? What new stages have you experienced? What are the episodes of your life that mark the time since their passing? Remember, these are your stories and your chapters. Give each period or series of events a name as a way to honor your experience and to remind yourself that life goes on—and that meaning emerges when you tell your story.

Here are my chapters as an example:

- Chapter 1: Life with Mom

- Chapter 2: The Death of Mom

- Chapters 3–8: Life After Mom

- Chapter 9: My Children

- Chapter 10: The Death of David Jr.

- Chapter 11: Life After David

1. _____

_____

_____

2. _____

_____

_____

3. _____

_____

4. _____

_____

_____

5. _____

_____

_____

Love Lives On: What You Take from Loss

At the end of the last chapter, I asked you to name the parts of your emotional life that you wanted to leave behind on your path to finding meaning, whether that was bitterness, anger, turmoil, or some other psychological states that might be keeping you from living a life of meaning.

Now it's time for the follow-up exercise. I'd like you to consider what you want to take with you from the loss. What are the things you'd like to carry into the future that you feel can serve you and support you in being the best possible version of yourself? What you left behind represents who you are now—the sticking points, the heavy emotions that keep you grounded. The things you want to take from the loss represent who you can be going forward. So much of grief is about feeling passive to it; it's something bad that happened to us. But this is a chance to get a little control back, to become active. Yes, grief happened to you, but you can also choose the parts of the experience that define your experience.

When someone dies, the relationship doesn't die with them. You have to learn how to have a new relationship with them. You can still keep learning from them in your everyday life. An instant will come up and remind you of something that happened between you and your deceased loved one, and now that they are gone, you can see it from a different point of view. As I get older, I understand my mother better because I've now lived longer than she did. I can see things from her side more than I ever could when she was alive, since I was too young to be able to do that.

I never leave the dead behind. I carry my mother with me. She lives within me. When a subject comes up, I might say something about what I think she might have thought about it. I bring the past into the present. I feel that I am still learning from her, which helps me go back and see the past differently. This is not only how our relationship continues to evolve and grow, it's also how I find meaning from my mother's love and from the loss that forever changed me. It's been decades since she died, but I still carry with me her zest for life, her sense of fun, and her curiosity. Likewise, with my son David, his spirit and love reside inside me. When I think of

David's sense of right or wrong, it becomes a moral compass for me. When I think of his compassion, it ignites mine. When I think of him not getting to be a helper, it is David who inspires me to fully embody helping others.

In death, our attachments continue, as does the love. Research regarding continuing bonds speaks to what I've seen in decades of work with bereaved people. Their connections stay with us, they guide and direct us, and those connections continue to evolve as we grow. I believe they are even wiser now. With that in mind, here are a few prompts to help you acknowledge the gifts of your loved one and how they live on within you. Taken together, these questions get to the heart of this work.

What are some qualities of the person who died that live inside you?

_____

_____

_____

_____

Share an example of a time you felt the continuing bond or connection to your loved one after their death. Did you ever experience a moment where you felt the person was with you or somehow connected with you? Please describe it.

_____

_____

_____

_____

What are some qualities of the person you'd like to carry with you going forward? Are there personality traits or behaviors of theirs that you'd like to internalize and somehow make your own?

_____

_____

_____

_____

Which parts of your emotional life do you want to take with you from the loss? Maybe it's an enduring sense of love or an emerging strength that comes with resilience. In the space below, reflect on how your relationship with the loss of your loved one is helping you evolve and grow.

_____

_____

_____

_____

_____

_____

What are some ways you can honor the person's life and their love with the gift of time you've been given since their death?

_____

_____

_____

_____

_____

_____

The Seven Questions

Since you're doing so well with these questions, let's go a little deeper. One of the most powerful exercises I do with groups is one framed around the Seven Questions. I share them here as a way to round out the work we've done together and to help you take a higher-perspective view of where you are in your healing process. Please take your time answering each of these questions. I really want you to think deeply about what this loss has meant in your life as you step forward with love in your heart.

1. What could death not touch? For example, *Death could not touch my love, or my connection.*

   _____

   _____

   _____

   _____

2. A part of you died with them, but what part of them lives in you? How can you foster and grow that part? For example, *My father was a generous tipper. I will be generous in restaurants.*

   _____

   _____

_____

_____

3. What beliefs or values did they possess, or what action steps did they take, that can help you in your grief and growth? For example, *They were kind. I could be kinder to myself.*

_____

_____

_____

_____

4. How can you recognize your survival strength? For example, *I am still here. I am showing up doing this workbook.*

_____

_____

_____

_____

5. What do you still have control over? For example, *I have control over my memories. How, where, and when I express my grief. How I live my life.*

_____

_____

_____

_____

6. What would your future self and your loved one want to see looking back on the rest of your life? For example, *I'd want them to see that I am grieving fully and living fully.*

_____

_____

_____

_____

7. What meaning can you find in their life and death that can heal you and honor them? For example, *Their kindness and generosity touched many people's lives. I'd like to continue that legacy by volunteering at my local food pantry.*

_____

_____

_____

_____

Constrictions and Expansions

My son David loved the work I did helping people facing death, dying, and grief. As I said at the start of this chapter, he never would have wanted his own death to constrict my life or my work in any way. Rather, he would have wanted me to expand in what I do and who I am. I feel that deeply. I try to live a happy, joyful life in honor of him.

That doesn't soften the pain of his loss or lighten the reality around death itself. I live with the fact that I'm going to die someday. Everyone we know is going to die someday. That can make me shut down, constrict, and go, "What's the point?" But I also have a choice. Having experienced loss, I can now say, "Let me take this in more." Let me not throw away this moment. Let me not throw away this day. Let me not throw away the rest of my life. Since I have a choice, my choice is to live in a profound, happy, and peaceful way. I miss my son and my parents, *and* I can still have an amazing life.

By expanding instead of constricting, we can all find meaning and joy in the pain. We can see that while loss is permanent, suffering is not. Physical death is forever, but your loss of hope is temporary. Even if you can't see a better future for yourself, I can see it for you. Until you can find hope again, I'm going hold hope for you. In fact, that's what this next mini-exercise is about. I'm going to help you find hope by giving you some action steps. Let's do it right now, you and me. Think of an expansion for yourself—a way to get bigger, stronger, or more engaged with the world in some way. As an example, I'll use "I would like to do more gardening." In the space on the next page, write down that expansion and an action or two you can take toward it. For me, maybe it's "buy and plant seeds" or "install a window-box garden."

Expansion	Action to Take
Do more gardening	Buy and plant seeds, install a window-box garden
Express my grief	Say my son's name, let people know it's okay to talk about those we miss
Honor my spouse's love for traveling	Take a trip to somewhere new

Expansion	Action to Take

Worry is not an action. Pain is not an action. Revolving self-blame in your mind is not an action. Sorrow is not an action. But by working through those states of mind, you propel yourself toward meaning. You grow where once you were stuck in your emotions. You expand where once you were constricted. This is how we honor our loved ones and make the most of the time we have in the here and now. I truly believe we owe it to them—and to ourselves—to live as fully as we can.

Letter to Your Future Self

Earlier in this workbook, I asked you to write postcards to yourself: one to your present self and another to your past self. You most likely wrote about your losses, the horrible wounds of yesterday, and how all those losses added up to your present state of grief. As we end this workbook, I'd like to conclude the way we do at some online and in-person events, and that's by having you write a letter about the future you envision for yourself. This is your letter to your future self.

The following page is blank. At the top, I'd like you to write: "The Future." That's it. Nothing else yet.

I sense you waiting for further instructions. That's what happens in my sessions too. Usually, I'll remain quiet until someone eventually asks, "Are you going to tell us what to write or give us some direction?"

"Sure," I respond. "Look at your paper. What do you see?"

Someone shouts out, "A blank piece of paper."

"Yes! *That* is your future," I say. "Blank. It isn't written yet. You are the author. You are the writer of your next story. You are no longer your past, not your losses, not death. But you. You are the creator of your future. Don't let your mind tell you otherwise. Your future is blank as of now. As the saying goes, 'Don't let your past dictate your future.'"

I'm sharing this now because I want to remind you that you still have every opportunity to find meaning. Even after all the pain you've experienced and the losses you've endured, you face the blank page of possibility. None of us knows what tomorrow will bring, but know that hope is a renewable resource. Hope is what keeps grief in check, and it gives us the energy and optimism to face another day and to find meaning.

I always like to point out that there's no meaning in a horrible death, just like there's no meaning in other losses, whether it's a divorce or a job loss or a move to another city. The meaning is inside us. It's what we find afterward. And that starts with a decision. Are you willing to find meaning in time? Are you willing to let yourself live a little more? Are you willing to think of ways that might honor what's happened with the loss in your life? It's a small decision but such an important one. Are you willing to grow? Are you willing to live past the traumas and pain you've experienced and see your remaining time here on earth as a gift?

It is my sincerest hope that this workbook has opened your eyes to new possibilities and helped you in your healing. But know there will be good days and bad days ahead. That's part of grief too. If you're struggling, reach out and get support. Talk to someone, whether it's someone who's been in grief themselves, a family member, a friend, or a counselor. Organizations like Grief.com, and so many other sites, have lots of free resources to help you. Look into my online grief group,

Tender Hearts. Maybe you even want to turn your pain into purpose in my Grief Educator Certification program.

Finally, I want to remind you not to be afraid of your feelings. As I said earlier, people think that if they start crying, they'll never stop. In all my decades of work, everybody stops eventually. It's okay to release those feelings in a healthy way. Those tears are evidence of love. Rest assured, no feeling is final, no feeling is forever. In time, my wish for you is to remember with more love than pain.

The Journey Forward
Meaningful Next Steps

So, what happens next? What do you do with all the insights and wisdom you've gained in these pages? Although this workbook has come to an end, our work together is not over. That's because meaning comes from doing. You know more about your pain and about your grief than when you started these exercises. My guess is that if you've come this far, you're ready to take some meaningful next steps.

There are so many ways to make meaning. You don't need to start a foundation or run a marathon in someone's honor. Tiny steps are just as meaningful. It could be cooking a meal for yourself. It might be taking a walk in a new neighborhood. You could volunteer at your church or synagogue, or meet someone for lunch who is recently bereaved. Maybe you've always wanted to learn to pour fancy designs in coffee like a barista. Developing a new skill like that is meaningful too.

I'll often say to people, "You have this one life remaining. This is it. What will you do with the opportunity?"

Lots of times I'll hear, "Well, I devoted myself to my marriage or my kids or my career or my friends or to the loved one who died."

That's when I'll tell them about the pie story I once shared in a book I wrote with Elisabeth Kübler-Ross called *Life Lessons*. There was a woman who said she thought of herself as a pie when she was a young girl. She gave a piece of her pie to her father, another piece to her mother, another to her sister, another to her brother. Then she got married. She gave a piece of pie to her husband and a piece to each of her two kids. When it was her time to die, she said, "I gave away so many pieces of pie, I never thought about which pieces were for me. What kind of pie am I?"

I encourage you to think about this. You still have your life. What are the things you've wanted to do but haven't yet done? Is there something you wanted to experience or see or discover as a child? Before you were married? Before this loss occurred? We all have a million dreams inside us. We're going to die with many of them unrealized. But I bet there are a few you actually could still achieve in this life. What's left of the pie for you to enjoy? Maybe it's getting better at tennis. Maybe you've always wanted to see the northern lights. Maybe it's going to New Orleans, New York, Los Angeles, Alaska, the Grand Canyon, London, Paris, Miami, Berlin. Whatever it is, it always starts with a tiny whisper in you that says yes to something. Start small if you need to. Do something nice for yourself. Go to the gym. Call a friend you haven't seen in a while. Spend time in nature.

Earlier in this workbook, we talked about grief bursts. Those are moments when you're doing okay and suddenly a big burst of grief comes over you. The next time it happens, I'd like you to consider whether the grief burst might actually be a love burst. Have you thought of that? When we're close to someone when they're alive, we sometimes, out of nowhere, get this feeling of love for them. That continues when people die. If you find yourself experiencing a burst of grief, think about it as a love burst, and you will find meaning in that too.

This loss has changed you forever. You can't go back to how things were before, but you can make meaning in how you live your life going forward. Recognize small accomplishments. Name your wins. Stop and pause for beauty when you notice it. I hope that doing this workbook felt like a win for you. Doing this is amazing, and I am so proud of you. I want you to embrace the ideas you learned here and apply them to your everyday life in ways that make you feel more connected, more grounded, more hopeful. Perhaps it will put you on a road to action. Or maybe it will be an ongoing source of comfort as your resilience grows, and you look back on these pages and the hard work you've done here.

Keep your eyes and your heart open but be good to yourself. I always tell people in grief, "no" is a complete sentence. You have the greatest excuse in the world. Someone has died. "Sorry, I can't do it." You get to say no and you don't have to explain yourself. Likewise, your address book should be by invitation only. Spend time with the people you want to spend time with. Life is too short to be obligated to people and experiences that don't serve you. At the same time, be open to connecting with people you haven't connected with. Be intrigued about people. Be intrigued about your friends, about old connections. I hear so many times with people facing loss that there's great meaning in reconnecting with old friends, reconnecting with friends from childhood. Many times, we yearn for connections. You may have had that one person who gave you so much of your emotional support. You may never have one person again in that same way, so think about how lots of people bring something to your life.

Even though you've had this terrible loss, it's still a beautiful world. It was beautiful for your loved one and is still beautiful for you. This is a radical concept. You may recall from *Finding Meaning* this concept of collateral beauty. We've all heard the term *collateral damage*. It's the damage that gets done in destruction. A bomb gets dropped on a target, but innocent people are killed. That's collateral damage. Collateral beauty is when something hideous happens, like a loss, but there is some beauty that comes out of it. I think about the people I met at some of the grief groups for parents who have become lifelong connections. I think about the people who cry and laugh with me at my speaking sessions. I think about you and the time and care you've put into this workbook. This is some of the collateral beauty that emerged from my losses. Can you find any beauty, any kindness, that's come out of yours?

You had something bad happen in the past. It's easy to be afraid of the future. But remember what you have control over is being present in this moment. Sometimes, I'll practice just naming five things in the room, naming three colors in the room, saying today's date out loud, and remember: *There is never going to be this day again.* You will never have this moment again. Do lots of things. Nourish your body. Put down the phone. Wherever you are, just be with yourself without wishing for more. In other words, be here now. You know the tragedy you've experienced, you know your loved one's physical journey is over. Their life ended, but yours has not. Maybe they continue to live through you, but at this point, your journey is the one that counts.

All those places, all those wishes your loved one had that were cut short—embody them, do them, and act upon your own wishes here and now. The poet Mary Oliver, who was an incredible person and writer, died a few years ago, but she continues to touch so many people with her words and ideas. Maybe her most powerful idea is a question I think all of us should ask: *What is it you plan to do with your one wild and precious life?* The person you love had a wild and precious life. Their physical journey is over. Now that wild and precious life is yours. Theirs was cut short. Yours is full of possibility and open to meaning. What meaning can you find in your wild and precious life? I hope that this workbook will continue to bring meaning as you move forward on your healing path.

About the Author

David Kessler is one of the world's foremost experts on grief and loss. His experience with thousands of people on the edge of life and death has taught him the secrets to living a happy and fulfilled life, even after life's tragedies.

He is the author of six books, including his latest bestselling book, *Finding Meaning: The Sixth Stage of Grief*. He coauthored two books with Elisabeth Kübler-Ross, *Life Lessons* and *On Grief and Grieving*, updating her five stages for grief. He also cowrote *You Can Heal Your Heart* with Louise Hay. He authored *Visions, Trips, and Crowded Rooms: Who and What You See Before You Die*. His first book, *The Needs of the Dying*, received praise from Saint (Mother) Teresa.

David's personal experience as a child witnessing a mass shooting while his mother was dying in a hospital helped him begin his journey. For most of his life, David has taught physicians, nurses, counselors, police, and first responders about the end of life, trauma, and grief. However, despite his vast knowledge of grief, his life was turned upside down by the sudden death of his twenty-one-year-old son.

David's volunteer work includes being a founding member of Project Angel Food, a well-known and loved nonprofit organization. He currently serves on the board of The Farrah Fawcett Foundation, which provides cancer research, patient assistance, and prevention efforts. He also serves as a specialist reserve officer for the Los Angeles Police Department and has served on the Red Cross's disaster services team.

His new online model of grief support, Tender Hearts, offers over twenty-five groups. Additionally, David leads one of the most respected Grief Educator Certification programs. He is the founder of Grief.com, which provides helpful resources to millions of visitors yearly from over 167 countries.